DISCOVER

by Doris Lockerman

A Comprehensive Guide to Its

ATLANTA

and Patricia LaHatte

* *Hotels, Motels, Restaurants and Night Life*
* *Annual Events and Sports*
* *Cultural, Educational and Health Facilities*
* *Convention Services*
* *Commerce, Industry and Transportation*
* *Churches, Clubs and Organizations*
* *Shopping and Services*
* *Residential Areas*

SIMON AND SCHUSTER *New York*

COPYRIGHT © 1969 BY DORIS LOCKERMAN AND PATRICIA LA HATTE
PUBLISHED BY SIMON AND SCHUSTER
ROCKEFELLER CENTER, 630 FIFTH AVENUE
NEW YORK, NEW YORK 10020

FIRST PRINTING

SBN 671-20210-3
LIBRARY OF CONGRESS CATALOG CARD NUMBER: 79-79635
DESIGNED BY IRVING PERKINS
MANUFACTURED IN THE UNITED STATES OF AMERICA

Contents

By skyway or roadway, come and embark on your own private adventure. Atlanta's airport is among the finest.

Atlanta's reflection of beauty is always partially in the eye and heart of the beholder.

Welcome to Atlanta

THERE IS no one image of Atlanta. Its seasons, moods, outlooks change constantly. It is many things to many people and no one sees it exactly as does his neighbor.

This fresh and prismatic quality accounts for the appeal Atlanta holds for its oldest citizens as well as relative newcomers.

A large and growing city has many facets. Its impact, as the reflection of beauty, is always partially in the eye and heart of the beholder. It inspires an emotion of participation.

We love Atlanta. We say so, loudly, clearly and often. Until someone chides us for our manners, we forget that this sentiment may not fall like music on the ears of all our neighbors to the north and south and even east and west.

A woman protested our chronic civic jubilation not long ago. "You act like your city is a person," she wrote. "Atlanta isn't exactly a human being, you know, it's just a big old pushy overgrown *place* in Georgia."

Well, Atlanta is a place, an irrepressible place, a beautiful place. It is a place that had to happen because Providence and who-knows-which cosmic force singled it out and signed it with an inexorable X.

That divine X is geography, climate, elevation; it is tall trees, fresh water, fertile soil; it is the song of birds, the cling of honeysuckle, the soft petals of flowers, the veils of mist caressing the valleys in the early morning.

But no X can be overgrown and pushy, and that's where people come in. Atlanta's people are proud, clear-eyed, high-spirited. If they appear sassy and striving to others, it's because audacity is braver than resignation and impudence is younger than smugness.

For Atlanta is young. For all its back-bending history, for all the soul-crushing heartbreak of its past, it is young and dewy-eyed and expectant.

Every day counts in Atlanta. Take your eye off it for a week and you'll miss something important. You may never catch up.

We admit that this introduction to Atlanta will not always be objective. It will present Atlanta as we see it. We invite you to set out with us; then embark on your own private adventure of discovery.

Phoenix, symbol of a city that rose from the ashes more beautiful than ever

Downtown Atlanta

Bird's-Eye View of the City

YOU MAY have glimpsed it from the south, the glinting arch of the capitol dome soaring into the sky like some Oriental mirage, and what surrounds it: the Romanesque curve of the Atlanta Stadium, and incredible logic of eighteen tentacles of interwoven interstate highways, the lofty consensus of a dozen government buildings, and, rising behind them all, an assembly of 20th-century business towers.

You had not known that Atlanta would be like this?

None of us did. We're still surprised.

That skyscape is a billion dollars' worth of enclosed space, arranged in layers of light and air and strength as glamorously as imagination and engineering could envision it. Beyond these will be a 70-story edifice still in the preliminary building stages. There are more, dozens more.

Most of this wasn't there ten years ago. Much of it wasn't there last year.

There are many places to take the measure of amazing Atlanta, but if you have a few minutes to spare, let's go to Five Points at the heart of the city and zip up to the

Atlanta Stadium, home of The Braves and The Falcons, lies in front of white marble governmental complex over which golden dome of State Capitol rises. Boxlike Archives Building is at right. Tallest building is First National Bank. City Hall is in center of photo. Intervening lacework is largest interchange east of the Mississippi, where three federal highways converge.

Top O' Peachtree in the National Bank of Georgia Building.

This is a restaurant. The decor is antebellum, the view is overwhelming. What you will see from the windows happened in only one hundred years.

You are standing approximately where a railroad surveyor pounded in a stake to connect the Western and Atlantic Railroad from Chattanooga with the Georgia Railroad from Augusta and the Central of Georgia from Savannah and Macon.

Before that the land belonged to the Creek Indians. They won the region south of the Chattahoochee River from the Cherokees as a trophy in a series of Indian ball games.

First, look south, toward the South expressway leading to the airport. You'll have to peer around the First National Bank, Atlanta's tallest building.

Just beyond, in the foreground, is the 24-karat dome of the State Capitol, covered with gold leaf—Georgia gold. Citizens of Dahlonega, 78 miles to the north, site of an early U.S. mint, brought these gold nuggets to Atlanta in a wagon train to give the dome its bright sheath.

To the right of the capitol you see Cherokee white marble-faced state office buildings. The marble came from Tate, 60 miles north. It's the same marble used in the Lincoln Memorial in Washington.

Nestled in among the governmental complex (the pale wedding-cake building is the City Hall) is the Roman Catholic Church of the Immaculate Conception, oldest Catholic church in Atlanta. It was reconsecrated as a shrine in 1954 by Archbishop Gerald O'Hara (no kin of Scarlett O'Hara's father). We'll tell you more about this church later.

Farther to the south, but out of your sight, is the Farmer's Market, the largest in the world.

Directly to the right and almost straight down is a patch of green—Plaza Park. It covers a railroad gulch. On the southwest corner, Peachtree Street begins. Now walk over and look toward the west.

You can see the South's largest department store, world-famous Rich's, which covers two city blocks connected by a glass bridge. The multi-leveled bridge is famous for the choral groups that serenade the city from its eminence at Thanksgiving time. On the same evening, a great tree atop the bridge is ceremonially lighted and the holiday shopping season officially begins.

Beyond, in the distance, are Atlanta University, Morehouse, Clark, Morris Brown and Spelman Colleges and the Interdenominational Theological Seminary. Atlanta has the largest facilities for higher education of Negroes in the world.

Now walk through the elevator corridor and look down Marietta Street to the Forsyth intersection. You'll see the Henry Grady monument, which impedes traffic a little but it's too significant to move.

On beyond the monument is the Federal Reserve Bank with its fine Ionic Corinthian columns standing as free as the pillars did in such historic places as Caesarea.

Glance to the north. On a clear day you can see Kennesaw Mountain and Lost Mountain. If you're a Civil War expert you'll know all about the Battle of Kennesaw Mountain and how many days it took to conquer this area before the actual battle of Atlanta could begin.

Also to the north is Lockheed, Georgia, where the world's largest airplanes, the unbelievable C5As, are being built.

You'll see skyscraper canyon forming as the taller buildings march out famous Peachtree Street. Notice how the railroads at left funnel into the city. That is why Atlanta happened.

Most of the railroad tracks have already been covered with plazas, parking garages and pocket-sized parks. Two new plazas are in the process of being developed; this will change the look and function of downtown Atlanta.

The Flint River actually rises deep beneath the earth where you are standing. It is safely capped and diverted southward, making its contribution to the beauty and fertility of mid-Georgia's broad and productive acres.

More than 20 streets in Atlanta have "Peachtree" in their names. Looking northward here over the first of the

Bird's-eye view of central downtown looking north. Beginning with the city's tallest skyscraper, First National Bank (1) towering over Five Points, the city's center, the buildings are: (2) pagoda-like First Federal Savings and Loan Association, (3) Atlanta Journal and Constitution, (4) Massey College, (5) Fulton National Bank, (6) old Post Office, (7) Equitable Life Assurance, (8) Peachtree Center complex containing Merchandise Mart, Peachtree Center Building, Twin Gas Towers, (9) Regency Hyatt House, (10) Life of Georgia, (11) new Trust Company of Georgia and (12) the old Trust Company, (13) Southern Bell Telephone and Telegraph, (14) Hurt Building, (15) Fulton Federal Savings and Loan, (16) Haverty Furniture, (17) Civic Center, (18) Heart of Atlanta Motel, (19) The Marriott Motor Hotel, (20) Landmark Apartments, (21) Holiday Inn, (22) Plaza Park.

Peachtree streets—its name *is* Peachtree Street—your view will be obstructed by a stunning group of buildings that have soared with the sixties and changed Atlanta's skyline completely: the 34-story Equitable Life Assurance Society Building: the 30-story Peachtree Center with three separate parallel wings; the 25-story Gas Tower with its twin tower; the 23-story Merchandise Mart with the new six-story Trailways bus station to its rear; the Georgia Power Company's 22 handsome stories; the Regency-Hyatt Hotel's 21 stories, and the Peachtree Towers Apartments with 24.

Old-timers who can remember way back to 1960 will gladly tell you about the beginning of the skyscraper blitz on Peachtree and what these buildings have replaced.

Now walk to the right and look out the windows to the east. Stone Mountain looms in the distance, a very old mountain geologically. It's a monadnock, worn down to bare granite, not thrust up like newer, upstart mountains. Among its attractions are the Confederate Memorial carving and the eleven-building Plantation complex, a retelling of a way of life (see page 90 for more on Stone Mountain).

The green-towered mission-type building is the Southeastern headquarters of Sears, Roebuck and Company. The beige structure in the foreground with the radar on top is the Southern Bell Telephone Company building.

To the right of the telephone building in your panoramic vision is massive Grady Memorial Hospital, named for the prophet of the New South whose monument you have already seen.

All around you, on the streets leading to Five Points are places of significance and memory in Atlanta.

Decatur Street, straight ahead, is a medley of pawn-shops, taverns, unmuted music and apothecaries where love potions have long been available to those with the misfortune to need them.

There is Big Bethel African Church, the largest Negro church in the south. It is on Auburn Avenue. It is more than 100 years old and at last count had presented its fire-and-brimstone Biblical pageant of sin and redemption, "Heaven Bound," to an appreciative public something like 800 times.

On the corner of Whitehall and Alabama Streets is the Old Lamppost, a relic of the War Between the States. It was first lighted on Christmas day, 1855. At its base is a hole torn by a shell during the siege of Atlanta in 1864. It now burns as a memorial to the old South.

You can't get to know Atlanta in five minutes. There are so many ghosts and shadows to be identified, so many questions to be asked and answered, so many private searches to be carried out.

So stay a little longer.

If You Have Five Hours

Atlanta hospitality is exactly as it was in the days of Ashley Wilkes and Scarlett O'Hara. Person to person. Doors fling open when knocked upon. The welcome depends on who does the knocking and who opens the door. Charm begets charm. Here, as elsewhere, hospitality is stronger if it isn't strained too much.

If you have a few hours to spare, you have two choices. You may take a walking (or driving) tour downtown and feel, at the end, that you have a pretty good idea of the area. Or you may decide to use the time to get a broader picture of the whole city.

If you want the latter, the Atlanta Transit Company conducts daily tours that originate at 1 P.M. at Broad and Peachtree. The bus will pick you up at downtown hotels or motels. The tour, which takes about four hours and fifteen minutes, should have you back where you started not later than 5:15 P.M.

The Charter Department of the Transit Company will arrange special tours for groups of more than 20 with just a little advance notice. The number is 524-2492.

If you take the transit tour, it will introduce you to the

Cyclorama at Grant Park, the special places of visual interest at Stone Mountain, the campus of Emory University, Lenox Square Shopping Center, the fine residential sections of Atlanta's north side, Peachtree Street with its historic markers, the Atlanta Historical Society's Swan House, ending with a whirl through Georgia Tech's campus and back to your starting point.

Gray Line Tours also offers five different tours, including one night excursion. Detailed information may be obtained by telephoning 524-6086.

If you choose to make it on your own and on foot, Five Points is a good place to begin.

WALKING TOUR DOWNTOWN ATLANTA

(1) Five Points, geographical center—First National Bank, National Bank of Georgia, Top of Peachtree Restaurant
(2) Federal Reserve Bank, Weinberg Eagle Sculpture
(3) Henry Grady Monument
(4) Rich's, Inc.—two stores connected by glass multi-layered bridge
(5) Atlanta City Hall
(6) Georgia State Capitol, area of state office buildings
(7) Atlanta Stadium
(8) State Archives
(9) Historic Lamppost
(10) Roman Catholic Church of the Immaculate Conception, Central Presbyterian Church nearby
(11) Hurt Park—opposite old Municipal Auditorium
(12) Georgia State College
(13) Grady Memorial Hospital
(14) Old Trust Company of Georgia, new nearby
(15) Commerce Building
(16) Greyhound Bus Terminal
(17) Trailways Bus Terminal
(18) Davison's Department Store
(19) Atlanta Public Library
(20) Merchandise Mart (Top of the Mart Restaurant) and Peachtree Center complex connect by sky bridge over Peachtree to Twin Towers (Atlanta Gas Light Co.)
(21) Regency Hyatt House
(22) Marriott Motor Hotel
(23) Holiday Inn—Central
(24) Heart of Atlanta Motel
(25) Terminal Railway Station
(26) Civic Center Complex
(27) St. Joseph's Infirmary
(28) First Methodist Church
(29) All Electric Georgia Power Building
(30) American Motel
(31) Dinkler Plaza Motor Hotel

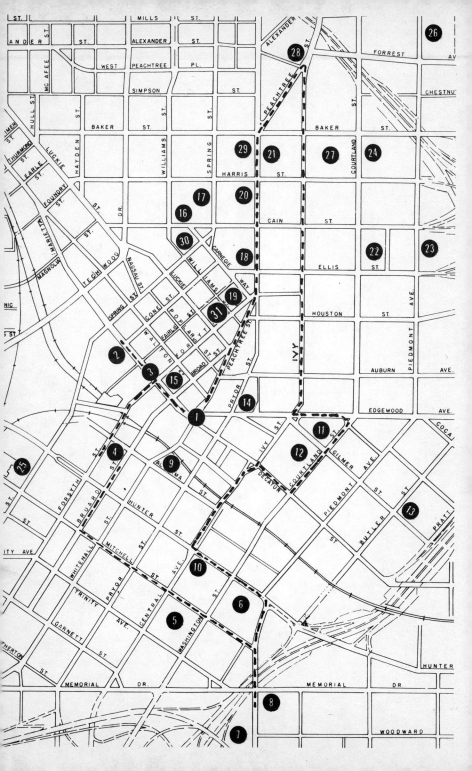

Walking Tour

Five Points is in the heart of the financial district, the asterisk on Atlanta's map where many things begin and end. This is not only Atlanta's money street, it is the equivalent of Piccadilly Circus as well; many notables have passed through it in review in one or another of the city's rousing parades.

First stroll up Marietta Street to the west and gaze at the Grady monument. Henry Woodfin Grady, editor of the *Atlanta Constitution* in the Reconstruction period, characterized the new South as a region too busy to hate. He said and wrote many other inspiring phrases in a very short lifetime, but those were his finest words. We are still fulfilling his visions.

Monument to Henry Woodfin Grady, prophet of the New South. Seated figures are Memory and History.

Continue west to the Federal Reserve Bank, one of Atlanta's most impressive structures, where Elbert Weinberg's 18-foot, ton-and-a-half, cast-bronze eagle is poised on a 48-foot free-standing column. Tensed for flight, it might be a phoenix rising from the flames. The phoenix is Atlanta's talisman, symbolizing the city's resurgence from the conflagration set off by General Sherman.

With its lyrical grouping of columns, solid, purposeful and strongly based, this building says exactly what should be said about the city.

The late Henry Toombs, who designed this building, used to grumble in the public press that "Atlanta is a terribly ugly city," but everybody knew he'd been having a love affair with the town for years.

Atlanta has a thriving School of Architecture at the Georgia Institute of Technology, more than 85 practicing architectural firms and 300 or more individual architects, all immersed in blueprints and budgets. These people have been saying deprecating things about Atlanta's commercial streets for at least two affluent decades, but we have not taken their criticism too seriously. We have sensed it was tempered with pride.

But we begin to see what they meant. Downtown Atlanta, "never planned for more than a cowpath," now has land-use plans, official zoning and builders who care for such factors as proportion, texture and suitability.

In the course of our recent phenomenal building boom, we have become conscious of flow and spatial relationships, interior design, outdoor furnishings, mass, color, relief, light and landscaping.

The Federal Reserve Bank stands on the site of Atlanta's

Cast bronze eagle by Elbert Weinberg weighing 3,000 pounds rests atop the tallest of five free-standing original columns of the Federal Reserve Bank. It is one of three sculptures by Weinberg in the city.

first mercantile business, the general store of Johnson and Thrasher. Here, too, was the home of Atlanta's first baby, Julia Carlisle, who made her appearance on August 17, 1842.

Wonder why Marietta Street is so wide? Credit it to straightforward, if informal, planning. The story goes that a founding father named Reuben Cone cut down the trees in this area so he could see from his house who was visiting Wash Collier's store. Collier, Atlanta's first commercial trader, had his store at Five Points, where the William Oliver Building now stands.

People started using the cleared area as part of the street, and these two blocks of Marietta have been wide ever since.

Walk back to the corner of Forsyth and Marietta Streets and you are at Massey Junior College. It has plush classrooms, libraries, even a roof garden, and fetches students to and from classes in the school's two double-decker London buses, Piccadilly Peach and Piccadilly Pete.

Across the street is the site of the law offices of the young attorney Woodrow Wilson in the years 1882 and 1883. The First Federal Savings and Loan Building has set up a Woodrow Wilson room on the second floor, complete with Wilson memorabilia of the days before he was 27th President of the United States.

Turn right and pass the Atlanta Newspapers Building, one of the city's early skyscrapers, where the *Atlanta Constitution* and the *Atlanta Journal* are jointly published and housed. The newspapers' promotion department conducts tours of the plant upon appointment in advance, usually for groups. Some exceptions are made for individuals if a guide is available.

You'll see the desk that Margaret Mitchell, author of *Gone With The Wind,* used when she began her reporting career with the *Atlanta Journal* Magazine. Notice the brass cannon on the 5th floor, fired in celebration when Grover

On the second floor of this First Federal Savings and Loan Association Building is the re-creation of Woodrow Wilson's law office which he had at this site in his youth.

Cleveland, a Democrat, finally took office after the Civil War. Above the cannon are front pages covering such historic events as the sinking of the *Titanic*, McKinley's and Kennedy's assassinations, World Wars I and II peace declarations and others of stirring memory.

Next door to the Atlanta Newspapers Building is the Union Station. It was built in 1930 at a cost of $600,000. At the height of the depression, it was heralded as one of the finest stations in the south.

The Terminal Station, on Spring Street to the right of Forsyth was opened for use in 1905 to the strains of "Dixie" and, of all things, Chopin's funeral dirge. The lament was not for the station, which was considered elegant beyond belief, but for some employees who had been relegated to an older building.

The next stop on Forsyth Street will be Rich's Store for Homes. If you have time, visit the decorator rooms on the 4th and 5th floors, the Connoisseur Gallery of antique furnishings on the 5th, and the Fine Arts gallery on the 3rd floor.

Walk across the Glass Bridge, through the Store for Fashion. When you emerge on the other side you will be on Broad Street.

Walk right to Mitchell, then left past the City Hall. It was built in 1929 of terra cotta, its main entrance and lobby walls finished with Georgia travertine. The bronze doors of the elevators are inscribed with the seal of Atlanta, a phoenix and the legend "Resurgens, Atlanta, Ga., 1847–1867."

This was the site of General Sherman's headquarters in 1864.

From here you can see the Fulton County Courthouse, where you are welcome to visit courts if they are in session.

You will notice the cluster of white state office buildings surrounding the Capitol. The Education Building is ornamented with six bronze relief figures, embossed on black marble spandrels, by Atlanta's sculptor, Julian Harris.

The State Capitol on Washington Street, between

Mitchell and Hunter Streets, is a copy of the National Capitol. It is built of Indiana limestone; the hallways and rotunda are finished in Georgia marble.

Busts and portraits of great Georgians, including those of Button Gwinnett, George Walton and Lyman Hall, signers of the Declaration of Independence, are set on columns around the rotunda of the Capitol.

The Capitol dome rises 237 feet above ground and may be reached by a staircase from the top floor of the building. The Georgia State Museum has its exhibitions arranged in the corridors of the upper-floor areas. The exhibits include displays of natural resources, minerals, fossils, Indian relics, birds, serpents and small animals, as well as dioramas of historic locations.

Notice the statues of Eugene Talmadge, Thomas E. Watson and Benjamin H. Hill on the square. The small Statue of Liberty was a gift of the children of France.

The State Library may be visited on the third floor.

If you happen to be here in January and February, the General Assembly may be in session. That's a show in itself.

Don't miss the Capitol landscaping. The buildings and grounds are under the care of the Secretary of State. In recent years, Secretary Ben Fortson has had a gun in his office which he has used on occasions to shoo away flocks of starlings that frequently threaten to take over the premises.

Walk up Capitol Avenue. Turning right, you will see the Fulton County Juvenile Court and Child Treatment Center and just beyond it, Atlanta Stadium, home of the Braves, Falcons and Chiefs.

Turn back and stop at the new Archives Building on your right. This is worth a real visit. If you can't do anything else, peek in the Assembly Room at the hand-carved staircase, backed by stained glass Confederate windows. They came from the A. G. Rhodes "Bavarian" mansion, erstwhile home of the state archives, now an outpost of this department of the state.

*Gold-leaf dome of State Capitol at right. Directly behind is the
Central Presbyterian Church with the Roman Catholic Church of
the Immaculate Conception behind it. To its left is the new Fulton*

County Courthouse Building with old courthouse behind. At extreme left is Atlanta City Hall. Judiciary Building and other state office buildings, left foreground.

Head back north, turning on Hunter to pay your respects to the Church of the Immaculate Conception. The land on which it stands was deeded to the Roman Catholics in 1848. The present red brick-and-granite church replaced an earlier frame building damaged during the Battle of Atlanta.

This church, as well as the Central Presbyterian, Trinity Methodist and St. Philip's Episcopal, were saved from destruction by Father Thomas O'Reilly, pastor of Immaculate Conception. Father O'Reilly had ministered unselfishly to both Confederate and Federal troops wounded in Atlanta. General Sherman, himself a Roman Catholic, spared these churches in response to Father O'Reilly's pleas.

In this general area a huge development has been planned to cover the railroad tracks with a new "city," including, among other things a 1,000-room hotel, four office buildings, 1,500 apartments and a rapid transit station, all to cost developer Raymond D. Nasher $200 million.

Go up Central Avenue toward Decatur Street and environs. Just before you get to Decatur, you'll see the Hungry Corner, a wide place in the road, where at practically any hour of the day you can find a good strong handyman to do a spot of work just by driving by and indicating what you need. It's a kind of open air employment agency.

Don't be alarmed at the concentration of uniformed policemen in twosomes at this corner. Decatur Street is a pungent area where life jives right along, but the reason for the policemen is less sinister. The Atlanta Police Department is on your right. Officers fan out from this place at all hours of the night.

You are practically on the campus of Georgia State College. Georgia State, which is racing toward an enrollment of 10,000 students, is rapidly becoming a multi-platform college. Its high-rise buildings will eventually command nine city blocks, with elevated walkways connecting the buildings. Dr. Noah Langdale, its popular president, a scholarly ex-football star, is known to his admiring students as "Gorgeous George."

You are close to Grady Memorial Hospital, Atlanta's largest general hospital, from which ambulances with wailing sirens set forth day and night to bring in emergency patients. "The Gradys" was built in 1958, replacing an earlier charity hospital. Primarily tax-supported, and governed by the Fulton-DeKalb Hospital Authority, it is the principal clinical teaching facility of the Emory Medical School.

Nearby is a plaque reading "Zero Mile Post," followed by a graven legend. Directly under this sign and under this street a crude stone pillar marks the actual birthplace of Atlanta. The stone was rammed into the ground to establish the end of the railroad line that ran from Chattanooga to what is now Atlanta.

No self-respecting railroad fan (and we have many, all over Georgia) would rest content unless he had been photographed, garbed in his hobby-engineering suit, with his hand on the Zero Mile Post.

Zero Mile Post of Underground Atlanta. This crude stone pillar marks actual birthplace of Atlanta.

The Post is in a historic part of old Atlanta, a twilight world of warehouse trucks, stray cats and winos, a face of the city known only to a few natives. Before the advent of the automobile, when the buildings rose above the original street level and the congestion of the railroad tracks, these cobblestones clattered with horse-drawn carriages carrying fashionable people or the briefcase brigade of the late 19th century.

Townspeople held a torchlight parade through this section for President and Mrs. Grover Cleveland in 1887, a cavalcade that ended in a blaze of crystal and gilt at the Kimball House. Once Atlanta's grandest Victorian hostelry, the Kimball House has succumbed to progress and its site is now a parking garage.

The Atlanta Civic Design Commission, an architectural advisory group, has ambitious plans to restore these subterranean passages of original Atlanta to evoke their gaslighted gaiety of a century ago. What the planners would like to see here is a historic Old Town, a reconstruction of the horse-and-buggy days with both those items present.

You're close to the old Municipal Auditorium and practically in the middle of Hurt Park. You should see Hurt Park at tulip time in the spring or at night in the summer when the trees are illumined and the fountain is shimmering with light.

On your left on Edgewood Avenue is the Young Women's Christian Association.

Beyond it, at the corner of Pryor Street and Edgewood Avenue, you can see one of the entrances of the old Trust Company of Georgia building, crouched now beside its new 28-story companion. This columned, tiered, corniced, entablatured, staircased, majestic structure was designed by Chicago's famous designer of skyscrapers, John Wellborn Root, who was born and reared in Atlanta. When it was built by Joel Hurt, in 1892, it was referred to cynically by colleagues as "Hurt's Folly." But not for long.

Central Avenue has by now become Ivy Street, so you will continue north on Ivy. You will see the Southern Bell

Hurt Park at tulip time. Towering magnolias, azaleas and other plantings keep downtown beauty spot aglow.

Telephone Building, enclosing a monstrous web of wires and electronic impulse buttons that makes sense out of spoken communications all over the Southeast.

St. Joseph's Infirmary, a Catholic hospital, is on Ivy, and farther north are the Sacred Heart Catholic Church and Convent. The twin spires of Sacred Heart at night are sky jewels, which gleam beautifully for downtown apartment dwellers in a breathtaking cityscape.

Over to your right, where the three interstate highways intersect in a bewildering bucket of worms, is an upthrust of stone and mortar which only a few years ago was one of Atlanta's slums. Here now are the Marriott Motor Hotel, the Holiday Inn, the 22-story Landmark Apartments, several high-rise office buildings and who knows what else, all a testament to the city's urban-renewal program in continuing progress since about 1957.

Now turn left and walk back to Peachtree. Take it slowly. The climb is steeper than you expect.

You're going to visit Peachtree Canyon.

Peachtree Canyon is the covey of monuments to money in the vicinity of Baker and Harris Streets.

On the right is the Georgia Power Company building, with its turned-on, tuned-in water fountains splashing away on the veranda for the big welcome and its lobby alight with a blazing 30-foot diameter chandelier. Who's counting candlepower here?

People come for miles to see the Regency Hyatt. During the first months the hotel was opened, traffic jams at the entrance were crushing. Entering the topless lobby is like walking into Mount Whitney and finding it hollowed out at the top. The glass elevators, climbing up the shaft in full daylight like giant fireflies, couldn't begin to carry everybody who wanted to ascend the full 21 stories.

If a body so desired, he could register at this hotel, park, transact business at the Gas Tower or at Peachtree Center South, buy or sell at the Merchandise Mart, see a friend at Peachtree Center, dine sumptuously, go to the theater, take a long walk and never set foot on dear old Peachtree Street at all. That would be a calamity, however, because Peachtreet Street is probably the most famous and romantically renowned thoroughfare in the United States. We won't attempt to explain it; we just revel in it and give it currency.

The concentration of valuable concrete in this canyon is mostly the handiwork of architects Edwards and Portman in collusion with a mint of cash, mostly trademarked Texas.

If you wish to dine at the Regency Hyatt, you've got some choices to take. You can take the elevators to the Polaris Restaurant lounge which sits on top of the hotel like an unidentified flying object coming slowly to rest. (If you sit down in the Polaris, keep your belongings at hand. If you don't, you may find they've revolved to the other side of Atlanta, panoramically speaking, by the time you have finished your refreshment.)

You can remain on the first floor and try the Kobenhavn, a continental sidewalk café in the lobby, or go downstairs to Hugo's on the terrace level.

If it's a bar you're seeking, try Le Parasol, a saucer-shaped cocktail lounge suspended from a cable 21 stories above, or the Club Atlantis for supper and dancing with entertainment.

You won't go hungry in this area. The several buildings of Peachtree Center offer 15 places to eat, all under one roof, including the new, sleekly Danish Midnight Sun. Besides those, there are other good dining establishments close by.

Across the street at the Merchandise Mart you may have your choice of the first-floor Stouffer's or Stouffer's Top Of The Mart (these are counted in the Center's 15 restaurants). The latter is built around a lushly planted atrium and provides a breezy view of the city.

By now you have seen some upstabs of sculpture suggestive of geological formations in the pleasant courtyard of Peachtree Center. This is called "Renascence" by Belgian sculptor Robert Helsmoortel. Helsmoortel says his idea of sculpture is that it must be involved with life. "Renascence" is. People walk through it, children hide in it, and nobody in his right mind ever passes it without a comment, sacred or profane.

Other sculptures in the Peachtree Center complex include the tall stainless-steel work, with flames jetting from its pipes, which stands in front of the Gas Tower with its own reflecting fountain. It is the work of the Dutch brothers, Hans and Gerit Van de Bovenkamp.

There are also three Willi Gutman sculptures in this neighborhood, including "The Big One" and "The Blue One."

The Diplomat restaurant is close by, just to the rear of the Merchandise Mart. It serves hearty man-sized portions in opulent surroundings.

You'll have noticed the Capital City Club for its restrained and dignified demeanor. It's the oldest private club in Atlanta.

There is also a good cafeteria nearby, the S & W, on down Peachtree. Try its Chess Pie.

You're in a good shopping area here. J. P. Allen's, Regenstein's, Leon Frohsin's, all have their devoted well-dressed clientele.

Davison's, a Macy's satellite, is a beautiful department store providing, with commanding authority, clothing for all members of the family, as well as general household furnishings. Small shops, all respected Atlanta emporia, are anchored on both sides of the street.

You may also dine at Davison's. Its Charl-Mont restaurant is a favorite of women shoppers as well as businessmen during the luncheon hour.

When you get to Davison's corner, you are only a block from the Atlanta Athletic Club and another block from the Atlanta Public Library. The Atlanta Public Library has, among other things, an impressive collection of manuscripts and memorabilia of Margaret Mitchell, Atlanta's most cherished author.

The city's major movie houses are within Oscar-throwing distance.

If you are going back to Five Points take Peachtree Street. It will take you past the new Equitable Building as well as the old Candler Building, back to the corner whence you started.

Lest you think Atlanta was born yesterday, the Candler Building, built in 1906, was the first skyscraper financed by Atlanta citizens with Atlanta money and constructed from Georgia material. This "20th Century Business Castle" cost the remarkable Asa Candler $1,000,000 of his Coca-Cola cash.

Back at Five Points, you might like to make a small

detour. Go a block to your right to the Commerce Building, where the Atlanta Chamber of Commerce will be glad to greet you and tell you how great Atlanta really is.

If you're interested in one man's colorful, if prejudiced, point of view, ask for Opie Shelton, the Chamber's executive vice-president. If you prefer the printed word, pick up a copy of the Chamber's award-winning publication, the *Atlanta Magazine*. The Chamber also has a selection of folders, pamphlets, booklets and maps for the information and direction of visitors.

The Commerce Club, in the Commerce Building, is Atlanta's most majestic private men's club. With a touch of apartheid, its founder, Mills B. Lane, decreed it off limits to women, except on Thursday nights when they are tolerated in the sacrosanct company of member males. One evening at the club, however, and women usually forgive Mr. Lane his intransigence.

As penance, Mr. Lane has opened a section of the Commerce Club's branch in the Citizens and Southern Bank's North Avenue Branch to women for luncheon. It also welcomes them five evenings a week.

Exhausted?

You still haven't seen the city's renowned residential section or the fine Negro University Center. You haven't seen Swan House or the Governor's Mansion. You haven't cuddled a baby chimpanzee at the zoo. You haven't seen a golf course, a lake, an arena, a tennis court, a swinging night club or a sultry saloon.

We're going to tell you about all these things in greater detail in subsequent chapters.

Check in at a hotel or reserve a relative's four-poster.

This is only the beginning.

Civic Center complex with exhibition hall at right connected to auditorium-theater on the left. Fountains play in the center. Vast parking area surrounds the structure, which is a short cab ride from central business district.

Convention
Information

WE LOVE conventions.

Atlanta is more readily accessible by air than any other city in the country. Two-thirds of the population of the United States is within two and a half hours by jet plane.

In an average year we entertain 300,000 conventioneers, so we're prepared.

Atlanta has well over 15,000 hotel and motel rooms with more a-building all the time. Within a three-block radius there are 4,000 first-class rooms.

We have 80 restaurants with a wide range of cuisines and more than 60 nightclubs and lounges.

Atlanta's Civic Center, the city's new auditorium complex at Piedmont and Forrest Avenues N.E., offers 70,000 square feet of air-conditioned exhibition space. This can be utilized for temporary seating of 11,500 persons, 600 exhibition booths or a banquet handling up to 7,000 persons seated at dinner.

The Civic Center includes a theater with 4,560 upholstered seats and a stage designed to handle the biggest of traveling companies. The auditorium can function as opera house, motion-picture theater, Broadway music hall, legitimate theater or lecture hall.

The Center's auditorium is connected to a column-free, two-acre exhibition hall by a lower court and passageway which provides subdividable space for smaller meetings and a kitchen designed to cater to 400 people.

The complex is within walking distance of all downtown hotels and motels.

The Municipal Auditorium, which when new rang with the crystalline notes of such celebrities as Metropolitan Opera star Geraldine Farrar, will continue to serve for a while as the setting for ice shows, basketball games, high school graduation exercises, the indoor Shrine circus and such meetings as spill over from the new Civic Center.

The Atlanta Merchandise Mart, second-largest trade center in the nation, has 2,000,000 square feet of exhibition and permanent showroom space.

The Atlanta Convention Bureau, 230 Peachtree Street N.W., a member of the International Association of Convention Bureaus, has been operating in Atlanta since 1913 as a civic, nonprofit agency.

The Convention Bureau serves as liaison between guests and the Atlanta business and service community, giving information, making arrangements, meeting unexpected problems.

Among many other services, the Convention Bureau has a list of historic Atlanta homes, some of which are open to visitors from time to time. The Women's Committee of the High Museum of Art sponsors a guided tour for busloads of 40 or more persons as a fund-raising project for the Museum. Other groups undertake the same service. There are limousine and walking tours of homes and communities, varying with the seasons.

If you wish, every detail of the convention can be turned over to an organization called the Complete Convention Services, Inc., 878 Spring Street N.W.

CCS will set up sales meetings, provide speakers, theatricals, visual effects, original music scores tailored to

Red, gold and glitter add sparkle to the lobby of the auditorium-theater of the Atlanta Civic Center.

corporate and marketing aims; will design sales-promotion programs; arrange transportation for your group; set up exhibits and booths; prepare printed material and do advance mailings; prepare visual aids of every kind; give information; take messages; do publicity and arrange tours and special events.

In addition to all this, CCS will park wives and keep them busy with special arrangements—free.

Atlanta's massive Merchandise Mart fronting on Peachtree Street in downtown Atlanta contains 2,000,000 square feet of exhibition and showroom space.

Hotels and Motels

WE HAVE homes away from home in every shape, size and price range.

The two largest downtown hotels are the Regency Hyatt House with 1,000 rooms and the Marriott Motor Hotel with 800 rooms. A third, the Royal Coach Motor Inn, now under construction, will also have 800 rooms.

Hostelries in this city have always been appreciated by residents as well as travelers.

For example, the Whitehall Inn of 1835 had a plank fence to keep out livestock, panthers and bears, but cash customers were entitled to a drink on the house. Well-mannered strangers left a nickel on the barrel head on the back porch after helping themselves to a shot of whiskey.

When the Whitehall expired, the Kimball House took its place. It was built in 1870 for $600,000 by Hannibal Ingalls Kimball, who was known in his time as a "steam engine in britches." The Kimball House welcomed four presidents with brilliant receptions and became the scene of glittering social affairs before it succumbed finally, a few years ago, to civic progress.

All hotels included in this guide book are air-conditioned and provide full guest services, including telephones in

View looking west, Landmark Apartments at right foreground. Among motels within easy walking distance of business district are, reading from right to left, Heart of Atlanta, Holiday Inn, Marriott and The White House.

Open lobby with greenery and a 70-foot fountain in the Regency Hyatt luxury hotel

Recent expansion of Marriott Motor Hotel provides second tower overlooking large swimming pool.

rooms, dining facilities, lounge or bar. They accept most major credit cards, including Citizens and Southern, Mastercharge, and BankAmericard. Most of them provide parking.

Following is a list of the principal hotels and motels arranged alphabetically by geographical location in three categories:

DELUXE:

Large convention facilities with exhibit space, meeting rooms, ballrooms, dining rooms, restaurants open 24 hours, bars and lounges with entertainment, night clubs, barber, beauty, gift shops.

EXCELLENT:

Less exhibition space than De Luxe, fewer shops, may not have all-night café, and may not provide entertainment in lounges.

GOOD:

Dining facilities, lounge or bar, meeting and display rooms.

Downtown

DELUXE:

Marriott Motor Hotel
Cain & Courtland Sts.
(30303)
Tel. 688-6500
800 rms. S. $15 up,
D. $20 up, each addl. $3;
suites $35 up; cots, $3.
Ck-out 2 P.M.

Regency Hyatt House
Peachtree Center (30301)
Tel. 577-1234
1,000 rms., S. $16 up,
D. $22 up; suites $50 up;
crib, cot, $4. Garage, $1.75
in and out. Ck-out 2 P.M.

EXCELLENT:

Admiral Benbow Inn
1470 Spring St. N.W.
(30309)
Tel. 872-5821
190 rms., S. $12 up,
D. $19 up; crib, rollaways
$2. Catering facilities.
Ck-out 3 P.M.

Atlanta American
Spring St. at Carnegie Way
(30303)
Tel. 688-8600
350 rms., S. $13 up,
D. $16 up, each addl. $2;
suites $40 up; crib, cots, $2.
Ck-out 2 P.M.

Atlanta Downtown
330 W. Peachtree St. N.W.,
at Simpson St. (30308)
Tel. 525-2771
103 rms., S. $10.50 up,
D. $13.50 up; cribs, $2,
cots, $3. Color TV. Pets.
Ck-out 3 P.M.

Dinkler Plaza Hotel
98 Forsyth St. N.W.
(Box 1702, zip 30301)
Tel. 524-2461
450 rms., S. $12.50,
D. $15 up; cot, $3. Garage.
parking, lounge, ent.
Display, sample rms.
Ck-out 3 P.M.

Downtowner Motor Inn
231 Ivy St. at Harris
(30303)
Tel. 577-1510
148 rms., S. $11.50 up,
D. $14 up; suites $25 up,
studio rms. $12.50 up;
crib, $1, cot, $2.50.
Heated pool. Pets. Dancing,
entertainment, meeting rms.
Ck-out 3 P.M.

Heart of Atlanta
255 Courtland St. N.E.
(30303)
Tel. 688-1682
216 rms., S. $14.50,
D. $16.50 up; each addl. $3,
under 12, $2; suites $18.50
up; crib, cot, $2. Color TV.
Two pools, one heated.
Playground. Coin lndry.
Meeting rooms, bar.
Ck-out 2 P.M.

Holiday Inn—Downtown
175 Piedmont Ave. N.E.
(30303)
Tel. 688-7420
253 rms., S. $12.50 up,
D. $16.50 up; suites $37.50
up, studio rms. $17.50 up;
crib free, cot, $2. Pool,
wading pool, playground,
kennel. Café, bars. Putting
green. Meeting room.
Ck-out, 2 P.M.

Inntown Motor Hotel
89 Luckie St. N.W. (30303)
Tel. 524-7991
73 rms. (more being added),
S. $14 up, D. $18 up;
crib free, cot, $2. Display
rooms, dining rm, bar, ent.
(Playboy Club in Hotel),
garage, pets. Ck-out 3 P.M.

Sheraton Biltmore
(formerly Atlanta Biltmore)
817 W. Peachtree St. N.W.
(30383)
Tel. 875-3461
645 rms., S. $14 up,
D. $19 up. Suites. Cribs,
cots, $3. Large exhibition
room and hall. Free parking.
Barber shop, beauty salon,
gift shops, drugstore,
dining rooms. Ck-out 4 P.M.

White House Motor Inn
70 Houston St. N.E. (30303)
Tel. 525-4201
220 rms., S. $16 up,
D. $20 up; suites $50 up;
under 12 free; Cot, $3.
Ck-out 2 P.M.

GOOD:

The Atlantan Hotel
Luckie & Cone Sts. N.W.
(30303)
Tel. 524-6461
300 rms., S. $8 up,
D. $10.50 up; suites $25 up;
crib free, cot, $2.
Free parking. Ck-out 5 P.M.

Georgia Hotel
114 Luckie St. N.W. (30303)
Tel. 525-3501
250 rms., S. $6.50 up,
D. $8.50 up; cot, $2.
No dining facilities, no
parking. Small meeting rms.
Pets allowed. Ck-out 4 P.M.

Hotels and Motels 53

Henry Grady Hotel
210 Peachtree St. N.W.
(30303)
Tel. 524-3211
500 rms., S. $10 up,
D. $14 up; suites $25 up.
Free parking. Convention
facilities, display rms.,
gift shop, sundries.
Ck-out 5 P.M.

Imperial Hotel
355 Peachtree St. N.E.
(30383)
Tel. 524-1941
150 rms., S. $7 up,
D. $11 up. Coffeehouse;
no dining rm. Ck-out 1 P.M.

Close In

EXCELLENT:

Albert Pick Motor Inn
1152 Spring St. N.W.
(30309)
Tel. 873-4361
210 rms., S. $11 up,
D. $15 up; suites $24 up,
family rates avail., crib, free,
cot, $2.50. Some oversize
beds, three wheelchair units.
Pool, pets. Ck-out 3 P.M.

Atlanta Cabana
870 Peachtree St. N.E.
(30383)
Tel. 875-5511
202 rms., S. $14 up,
D. $17 up, each addl. $2;
suites $40 up; crib, $1,
cot, $2. Pool. Pets. Café
(Switzerland House). Bar,
dancing. Meeting rms,
putting green. Ck-out 3 P.M.

Atlanta Central Travelodge
311 Courtland St. N.E.
(30303)
Tel. 524-8031
70 rms., S. $10 up,
D. $13 up, each addl. $2;
crib free, cot, $3. Heated
pool. Pets. Meeting rm.
2 units for handicapped.
Ck-out 1 P.M.

Atlanta Peachtree Travelodge
1641 Peachtree St. N.E.
(30309)
Tel. 873-5731
60 rms., S. $10 up,
D. $12 up, each addl. $1–2;
crib, $1, cot, $2.
Heated pool. Ck-out 1 P.M.

Georgian Terrace Hotel
659 Peachtree St. N.E.
(30383)
Tel. 872-6671
250 rms., S. $11 up,
D. $14 up; suites $25 up;
cribs free, cot, $4. Meeting,
display rms.; ballroom,
dining rm., bars.
Ck-out 3 P.M.

Holiday Inn—Central
1944 Piedmont Circle, N.E.
(30324)
Tel. 875-3571
163 rms., S. $11 up,
D. $15 up, each addl., $2;
suites $39 up; under 12 free;
crib free, cot, $2. Pool.
Kennel. Meeting rms.
sundries. Ck-out 2 P.M.

Holiday Inn—Northwest
1810 Howell Mill Rd. N.W.
(30325)
Tel. 351-3831
207 rms., S. $10 up,
D. $12 up, each addl. $2;
suites $50 up; under 12
free; crib free, cot $2.
Heated pool. Playground,
kennel. Café, meeting rm.,
bar. Ck-out 12 noon.

Howard Johnson's Motor Lodge
—Northwest
1701 Northside Dr. N.W.
(30318)
Tel. 351-6500
108 rms., S. $12 up,
D. $15 up, each addl. $2;
kit. suites $28 up; under 13
free; crib, $1, cot, $3. Pool,
wading pool. Playground,
kennel. Café. Bar, rm. serv.,
coin lndry. Meeting rms.,
sundries. Ck-out 2 P.M.

Howard Johnson's Motor Lodge
—South
759 Washington St. S.W.
(30315)
Tel. 688-8665
210 rms., S. $13 up,
D. $16 up, each addl. $1;
suites $35 up; under 12
free; crib, $1, cot, $3.
Pool, wading pool,
playground, kennel. Café,
rm. serv., bar. Coin laundry,
meeting rms. Ck-out 2 P.M.

Mark Inn—Northwest
1848 Howell Mill Rd. N.W.
(30318)
Tel. 351-1220
64 rms., S. $12 up,
D. $14 up, each addl. $4;
crib, cot, $2. Heated pool,
wading pool. Café, rm. serv.
Coin laundry. Meeting rms.
Ck-out 12 noon.

Hotel Bel-Air and Racquet
Club
2140 Peachtree Rd. N.W.
(30309)
Tel. 355-7771
68 rms., S. $10 up, D, $14 up;
rollaways, cribs, $3.
Ballroom, dining rm.; Pool.
3 tennis courts, health club,
terrace dining for
swimmers, tennis players.
Meeting rms., lounge, ent.
Parking. Ck-out 3 P.M.

Riviera of Atlanta Motor Hotel
1630 Peachtree St. N.W.
(30309)
Tel. 875-9711
330 rms., S. $13 up,
D. $16 up; suites $39 up;
cribs, cots, $2. Dining rms.,
heated pool, ballrms.,
exhibit rms., coin laundry,
parking. Lounge with ent.
Barber, beauty shops;
Ck-out 3 P.M.

Rodeway Inn
144-14th St. N.W. (30318)
Tel. 873-4171
80 rms., S. $10 up,
D. $13 up.; studio rms.,
$15 up; crib free, cot $2.
Pool. Pets. Café, rm. serv.,
bar, meeting rms., sundries.
Ck-out 2 P.M.

Squire Inn Motel
2115 Piedmont Rd. N.E.
(30324)
Tel. 876-4365
124 rms. (35 being added),
S. $12 up, D. $14 up;
suites $25 up; cribs, $2;
rollaway beds, $3. Pets.
Rm. serv., valet, parking,
bars, ent. in lounge.
Dining rm. Large and small
exhibition rms.
Ck-out 2 P.M.

GOOD:

Briarcliff Hotel
1050 Ponce de Leon Ave.
N.E. (30383)
Tel. 874-9711
109 rms., S. $7 up,
D. $11 up; efficiencies and
suites. Ck-out 4 P.M.

Cherokee Motor Inn
310 Ponce de Leon Ave.
N.E. (30383)
Tel. 875-8401
66 rms., S. $7 up, D. $10 up;
suites $20 up; cribs,
rollaways, $2. Ck-out 2 P.M.

Cox-Carlton Hotel
686 Peachtree St. N.E.
(30383)
Tel. 872-7721
139 rms., S. $7.50,
D. $10.50 up; cribs free,
cots, $2. Ck-out 4 P.M.

Howell House
710 Peachtree St. N.E.
(30308)
Tel. 873-4821
535 rms., S. $12 up,
D. $15 up; suites $13 up;
cribs, cots free if for
under 12. Ck-out 2:30 P.M.

Peachtree Manor Hotel
826 Peachtree St. N.E.
(30334)
Tel. 874-2791
65 rms., S. $8 up,
D. $10.50 up; suites $14 up.
Ck-out 4 P.M.

Pershing Hotel
1428 Peachtree St. N.E.
(30384)
Tel. 892-2050
103 rms., S. $8 up,
D. $12 up; suites $16 up;
cribs, cots $2. Ck-out 3 P.M.

551 Ponce de Leon Hotel
551 Ponce de Leon Ave. N.E.
(30383)
Tel. 872-4721
50 rms., S. $6 up, D. $8 up,
cots, $2. Ck-out 1 P.M.

Tech Motel
120 North Ave. N.W.
(30313)
Tel. 873-3721
82 rms. (40 being added),
S. $10 up, D. $12 up;
under 12 free.
Pool, playground.
Ck-out 2 P.M.

Outlying

NOTE: Only motels rated Excellent are listed for the outlying areas. Most of these have pools, playgrounds, restaurants, bars, coin laundries, or these are available nearby. Most have meeting rooms, room service. Most accept pets. All have free parking.

NORTH, NORTHWEST, NORTHEAST, EAST

Dinkler Belvedere Motor Inn
3480 Memorial Dr.,
Decatur (30032)
Tel. 289-6633
100 rms., S. $7.50 up,
D. $9.50 up, each addl. $3;
crib, $1.50. Ck-out noon.

Executive Park Motel
1447 Northeast Expressway,
N.E. (30329)
Tel. 634-4231
250 rms., S. $13 up,
D. $16 up, each addl. $2;
suites $41 up; crib, $1,
cot, $3. Ck-out 2 P.M.

Dogwood Motel
5140 Buford Hwy.,
Doraville (30040)
Tel. 457-7246
61 rms., S. $7.50 up,
D. $9.50 up; crib, $1,
cots, $2. Ck-out noon.

Golfland Motor Lodge
3701 Northeast Expressway,
Doraville (30040)
Tel. 451-4811
106 rms., S. $10 up,
D.·$14 up; cribs free,
cots, $2. Ck-out noon.

Holiday Inn—Northeast
4423 Northeast Expressway,
Doraville (30040)
Tel. 457-6301
112 rms., S. $10, D. $14.,
each addl. $2; crib free,
cot, $2. Ck-out noon.

Howard Johnson—Northeast
2090 N. Druid Hills Rd.
(30329)
Tel. 636-8631
160 rms., S. $14 up,
D. $17 up; cribs free,
cots, $3. Ck-out 2 P.M.

Mark Inn—East
279 Moreland Avenue, S.E.
(30316)
Tel. 524-1281
54 rms., S. $10 up,
D. $16 up; suites $24 up;
crib, cots, $2. Ck-out noon.

Northwoods Motel
5114 Buford Highway,
Doraville (30040)
Tel. 457-5221
25 rms., S. $8 up, D. $10 up;
cribs, cots $2. No rm.
service. Ck-out noon.

Ramada Inn
2960 N. E. Expressway,
Chamblee (30005)
Tel. 451-5231
160 rms., S. $11 up,
D. $16, each addl. $2;
crib free, cot, $2;
studios $16 up. Private club,
dancing, putting green.
Ck-out noon.

Rodeway Inn—Clairmont
706 Clairmont Rd. N.E.
(30033)
Tel. 634-6291
120 rms., S. $12 up,
D. $16 up; suites $28 up,
each addl. $2; cribs free,
cots $2. Ck-out 3 P.M.

Rodeway Inn—Lenox
3387 Lenox Rd. N.E.
(30326)
Tel. 231-5500
116 rms., S. $11, D. $16,
each addl. $1; suites $20 up;
under 12 free; cribs free,
cot, $2. Ck-out 2 P.M.

Stone Mountain Inn
Stone Mountain Memorial
Park (30083)
Tel. 469-3311
90 rms., S. $10.50 up,
D. $12.50, each addl. $1;
crib free, cot, $1.
Ck-out noon.

Sheraton Emory Inn
1641 Clifton Rd. (30329)
Tel. 636-0341
114 rms., S. $12 up,
D. $16 up; suites $32 up.
Ck-out 3 P.M.

Airport and South

Air Host Inn
1200 East Virginia Ave.,
Hapeville (30301)
Tel. 767-7451
310 rms., S. $12.50 up,
D. $15.50 up, each addl. $3;
suites $25 up; special
between-plane nap rates;
crib free, cot $3. Health
club. Free airport bus.
Ck-out 3 P.M.

American Host
3999 South Expressway,
Hapeville (30354)
Tel. 767-9741
103 rms., S. $9.50 up,
D. $10.50 up; suites $16 up;
cribs free, cots $2.
Ck-out noon.

Hilton Inn
1031 Virginia Avenue,
Hapeville (30301)
Tel. 767-0281
350 rms., S. $15 up,
D. $19 up; suites $50 up;
cots, cribs, free. Car to
airport, special day rates.
Ck-out 3 P.M.

Holiday Inn—South
South Expressway,
Hapeville (30054)
Tel. 766-7511
166 rms., S. $10 up,
D. $11 up, each addl. $2;
under 12 free; crib free,
cot $2. Ck-out noon.

Holiday Inn—Airport
1380 Virginia Avenue,
East Point (30320)
Tel. 762-8411
301 rms., S. $12 up,
D. $15 up, each addl. $3;
suites $55 up; studio rms.
$17 up; crib free, cot $2.
Ck-out noon.

Mark Inn—Airport
3118 Sylvan Rd.,
Hapeville (30054)
Tel. 762-8801
120 rms., S. $13 up,
D. $16 up; cribs free.
Ck-out noon.

Mark Inn—South
2750 Forrest Hill Dr.
(30054)
Tel. 767-2694
105 rms., S. $10 up,
D. $14 up, each addl. $3;
crib, cot, $3.
Free airport bus. Several
units for handicapped.
Ck-out noon.

Old South
331 Cleveland Ave. S.W.
(30354)
Tel. 767-7442
100 rms., S. $7 up,
D. $10 up; cribs $2,
cots, $2. Ck-out 1 P.M.

Sky Host Inn
1360 Virginia Ave.,
East Point (30320)
Tel. 761-5201
100 rms., S. $10 up,
D. $14 up. Airport bus.
Ck-out 3 P.M.

Waldorf Motel
4710 S. Expressway
(U.S. 19, 41, 75),
Hapeville (30054)
Tel. 767-8631
65 rms., S. $8 up, D. $11 up;
cottage $20 up. Cribs free,
rollaways, $2. Ck-out noon.

WEST

Mark Inn—West
4430 Frederick Dr. S.W.,
on Industrial Boulevard
(30336)
Tel. 344-9310
115 rms., S. $12 up,
D. $16 up; suites $30 up;
crib free, cot $2.
Bus to Fulton Co. Airport.
Ck-out noon.

Restaurants

SUCCULENT COUNTRY ham, melt-in-your-mouth biscuits, sweet-potato soufflé flicked with a trace of bourbon, chicken fricassee . . .

Whatever you mean by Southern cooking, it's here, but it's going to be hard to find outside a few lucky domains where the yams are still candied and the collards and crowder peas still simmer.

In most restaurants you'll run into Yorkshire pudding more often than spoon bread, crepes suzette more frequently than syllabub. If it's turnip greens with pot licker you're craving, try settling for broccoli with hollandaise. You'll have a better chance of finding it.

Atlantans are from everywhere, going everywhere. The city is not only the Great Exchange in the marketplace but a great melting pot-au-feu in the kitchen.

A recent article about virtuoso Atlanta cooking talked a great deal more about vintage wines, truffles, escargots, pâté de foie gras, continental cheeses than it did about Dixie-done chicken.

Businessmen of the city run a constant alert for the home-cooking bit in luncheon fare. Once in a while one of them finds the place where he can settle for vegetables and corn bread and an occasional bowl of berry cobbler, but these hideaways are too modest and unassuming even to have signs in front.

We have chosen a collection of the best restaurants from our point of view, and Southern cooking will please take its place in the list that follows.

Most of these restaurants have lounge or bar facilities, accept credit cards and appreciate reservations. Many close on Sunday. When you inquire about reservations, ask about dancing, if you are interested.

Continental and American Cuisine

* * * S U P E R L A T I V E

****Chateau Fleur de Lis*   N.E. Freeway and Lenox Rd., Tel. 633-2633
  Sleek, soigné, with dishes like Dover sole, for instance. No Sundays.

***The Diplomat   230 Spring St. N.W., Tel. 525-6375
  Big-time atmosphere with matching menu, for gourmets with gourmand tendencies.

****Justine's*   3109 Piedmont Rd. N.E., Tel. 233-7129
  Polished and assured; in a restored 18th-century manor house. Dinners only. No Sundays.

Justine's on Piedmont Avenue offers both architecture in the Southern style and gracious dining.

The Midnight Sun Terrace, Peachtree Center S., Tel. 577-5050
  New Danish stunner, continental menu with such specialties as Royal Rack of Lamb and Danish Curry Pot. Luncheon and dinner. No Sundays.

Saccone's 1232 West Paces Ferry Rd. N.W., Tel. 233-3211
  Suave setting for fine fare. Fresh seafood specialties; also steaks.

The Coach and Six 1775 Peachtree Rd. N.W., Tel. 873-2741
  The favorite rendezvous of advertising and electronic-media personalities. Ask for the special Caesar salad or crepes suzettes.

Fan and Bill's W. Peachtree at Fifth, Tel. 876-7554
  All-embracing menu, very brisk service.

Herren's 84 Luckie St. N.W., Tel. 524-4709
  Atlanta's standard downtown reliable, year in, year out. Great lobster and beef. AND AN ART GALLERY.

Hugo's Regency Hyatt House, 265 Peachtree St. N.E., Tel. 577-1234
  One of the Regency's lavish and excellent tables.

The Little Mermaid Terrace Level, Atlanta Gas Light Tower, Tel. 577-5050
  Danish luncheon spot, delicious open-face sandwiches, crepes with various fillings. Mini-smorgasbord daily and Sunday. Danish pastries to take out. Open for breakfast and until 8 P.M.

The Pyrenees Room Sheraton-Emory Inn, 1641 Clifton Road N.E., Tel. 636-0341
  A varied menu with interesting continental touches, straight from Le Pays Basque.

The Rendezvous Sheraton-Biltmore, 817 W. Peachtree St. N.E., Tel. 875-3461
  Good salads made before your eyes, fruits, and Eggs Benedict, as well as stouter fare.

The Riviera 1630 Peachtree St. N.W., Tel. 875-8466
  Popular for lunch, with varied menu. Beef, seafood, fowl entrees at one price ($3.95) for dinner.

Stouffer's Bottom of the Mart   Merchandise Mart, 240 Peachtree St. N.W., Tel. 688-8650
   Stouffer's wholesome American food, quietly served.

Stouffer's Top of the Mart   Merchandise Mart—24th floor, Tel. 688-8650
   Excellent food served around a beautiful brick courtyard garden. Your own little loaf of hot bread.

Su Casa   The White House, 71 Houston St. N.E., Tel. 525-4201
   A lavish Iberian-American table.

Switzerland House   Cabana Motel, 870 Peachtree St. N.E., Tel. 874-3519
   If you're neutral about Swiss Dishes, try French or German ones here.

Top O'Peachtree   30th Floor, National Bank of Georgia Bldg., Five Points, Tel. 688-2475
   Good food and an overwhelming view of Atlanta.

Yohannan's   Lenox Square, Tel. 233-1191

Yohannan's Across the Street   3393 Lenox Road, N.E. Tel. 261-3491
   Yohannan's restaurants serve excellent strip sirloins, prime ribs, filets. Also things like crabmeat au gratin and a Sunday smorgasbord.

Chinese and Oriental

Eng's Gourmet   3707 Roswell Rd. N.E., Tel. 261-2596

Trader Eng's Hibachi Steak House   300 W. Peachtree St. N.E., Tel. 523-5822

House of Eng   Tenth St. at Peachtree N.E., Tel. 873-4704
   Chinese-American-Polynesian comestibles, all the standards and most of the exotics. Try marinated filet mignon, for instance.

Ding Ho Restaurant   26½ Cain St. N.E., Tel. 522-6706
   This is a second-floor walk-up with moderately priced Chinese food served family style. Lobster Cantonese lives here regularly.

Hong Kong   108 Luckie St. N.W., Tel. 523-5117
   The Char Shu Ding only makes you want more, so start with a bowl of Won Ton.

Italian

Biuso's   2975 Peachtree Rd. N.E., Tel. 233-9280
All the best Italian specialties, as well as Spanish fare,
American steaks and seafood.

Caruso's Italian Restaurant   1893 Piedmont Ave. N.E., Tel.
873-6583; also at 2496 Stewart Ave. S.W., Tel. 766-8561
Atlanta's largest Italian restaurants, varied menu with all
the pastas and pizzas as well.

Gene and Gabe's   1578 Piedmont Ave. N.E., Tel. 876-9426
Charming small Italian restaurant with a special flair for
veal dishes.

Salvatore's Neapolitan Restaurant   669 Peachtree St. N.E.,
Tel. 872-9161
Small trattoria with a hideaway feeling, across from the Fox
Theater, second-largest movie house in the world.

German

Old Heidelberg   3209 Maple Dr. N.E., Tel. 233-5338
Very *gemütlich* little restaurant with many specialties of the
house imported by the Hamburger family and prepared by
their own hands.

Jewish (Kosher If Requested)

Happy Herman's Sidewalk Cafe   Greenbriar Shopping Center
on the Mall, Tel. 344-5782
Barbecued and kosher sandwiches, pizza, fried chicken.

Nosh O'Rye   1965 Cheshire Bridge Rd. N.E., Tel. 876-1882
Such toothsome foods as cheese blintzes, potato pancakes,
lox, bagels, cream cheese and Roumanian steak.

Leb's Restaurant   66 Luckie St. N.W., Tel. 525-8648
A complete menu; Jewish dishes, sumptuous desserts; oyster
bar.

Beef and Steak Houses

Red Barn Inn 4300 Powers Ferry Rd. N.W., Tel. 255-7277
Charcoaled steaks served in pretend horse stalls.

Brave-Falcon Lounge 2329 Cheshire Bridge Rd. N.E., Tel. 636-4868
Great steaks and sandwiches.

Captain's Table Heart of Atlanta Motel, 261 Courtland St. N.E., Tel. 525-5678
Prime beef or fish.

The Chalet 2225 Peachtree Rd. N.E., Tel. 351-1630
Seafood and steak served in a Swiss atmosphere. Maybe even fondue, if you ask.

Dale's Cellar 400 W. Peachtree St. N.W., Tel. 522-9000
Informal atmosphere, formal steaks.

The Fourteen-O-Four 1404 Peachtree St. N.E., Tel. 872-9192
Beef and seafood.

The Golden Palm Atlanta American Motor Hotel, Spring St. and Carnegie Way, Tel. 688-5603
Roast beef, steak and Boeuf Bourgignon, all *au point.*

Lulubell's Steak House Hilton Inn (Across from Atlanta Airport), Tel. 767-0281
Not only steak, though that would be enough.

The Maid's Quarters 757 Piedmont Ave. N.E., Tel. 874-9156
Whimsical spot with interesting Beef Stroganoff, beef kabobs, Beef Burgundy.

Jimmy Orr's 2355 Peachtree Rd. N.E., Tel. 261-1568
Sports personalities congregate here with old teammate Jimmy Orr. If steak palls, try Eggs Benedict.

Prince George Inn 114 Sixth St. N.E., Tel. 876-9173
Beef dishes of all kinds, with steak a specialty.

The Red Baron's Inn 2139 Campbellton Rd. S.W., Tel. 753-9108
Hamburgers here are big. Steaks also.

The Regency Room Holiday Inn, 175 Piedmont Ave. N.E., Tel. 688-7420
Chateaubriand and filet mignon are casual fare in this house of beef.

The Round Table 2416 Piedmont Rd. N.E., Tel. 261-6825
Good ribs of beef, choice steaks, and brisk service.

The Sirloin and Saddle   Atlanta Marriott Motor Hotel, 165 Courtland St. N.W., Tel. 688-6500
>   Marvelous roast beef as well as other fare; and a dessert called Black Forest Cake to eat now, count calories later.

Squirrel Cage   1999 Peachtree Rd. N.E., Tel. 351-6747
>   Open-hearth steaks in a piquant atmosphere.

The Steaks   3539 Northside Parkway N.W., Tel. 233-1297
>   The name says it to standing-room only audiences. Family fare as well as succulent steaks.

The Three Hearths   Air Host Inn (at the Airport), Tel. 767-7451
>   Steaks, shish kebab and stuff, every day of the week.

The Town and Country   Dinkler Plaza Hotel, 98 Forsyth St. N.W., Tel. 524-2461
>   Good thick prime ribs, excellent beef dishes.

French

Emile's French Cafe   87 Fairlie St. N.W., Tel. 523-4428
>   Oldest French café in Atlanta. Try French pancakes with sour cream and fruit.

Fish

Cross Roads Restaurant   1556 Peachtree St. N.W., Tel. 875-2288
>   Lobster and shrimp heaven. Other fish too, of course.

Ye Olde Chesapeake House   243 Peachtree St. N.E., Tel. 525-5914
>   Chowders of all kinds are special here. Oysters are always in season.

British

The Lion's Head   1915 Peachtree Rd. N.E., Tel. 355-7130
>   Veddy British beef, cheeses, pastries, with Saturday a day for champagne-and-coddled-egg luncheons.

Ye Olde Bull and Bush   1905 Piedmont Rd. N.E., Tel. 873-5665
London broil, of course, fish and chips, steaks, typical tavern foods.

The George   315 W. Ponce de Leon, First National Bank Building (Decatur), Tel. 377-8168
18th-century pub/inn featuring steaks, triple-cut chops and seafood. Closed Saturdays and Sundays.

The Pewter Mug   38 Auburn Ave. N.E.
Beef in all modes, a good green salad and general tavern food.

Greek

The Iron Horse   1160 Peachtree St. N.E., Tel. 876-9564
Just the way they eat and serve in the old *tavernas* along the Aegean coast. Try the thin soup with lemon, dolmades—any kind they serve—and the richest pastries this side of Piraeus.

Mexican and Spanish

El Mexicano   634 Peachtree St. N.W., Tel. 876-7456
Chiles rellenos, tostadas, guacamole salad—anything Mexican, served with music, and with Mexican beer, if you ask for it.

Escoes   2143 Peachtree Rd. N.E., Tel. 355-0707
Spanish and Mexican menus, as well as delicious steaks and American goodies.

El Palacio   310 Ponce de Leon Ave., Tel. 872-9241
Mexican and American menu.

Southern Cooking

Aunt Fanny's Cabin   375 Campbell Rd. (Smyrna), Tel. 435-9131
The South has riz again and Aunt Fanny's done proved it.

Pitty Pat's Porch   25 Cain St. N.W., Tel. 525-8228
Old-fashioned and newfangled edibles, you-all atmosphere, supper dancing at 8:30 P.M.

Mammy's Shanty   1480 Peachtree St. N.W., Tel. 872-3551
  Such things as pecan pie, their own hot breads, corn muffins,
  Southern fried chicken and vegetables you can enjoy.

The Farm   3820 Roswell Rd. N.E., Tel. 237-7504
  All the dishes you'd hope for from a Georgia kitchen, if it
  were Grandmother's farm.

Plantation House Restaurant   5628 Memorial Drive (Stone
Mountain), Tel. 443-6457
  Robert E. Lee, Stonewall Jackson and Jeff Davis could have
  dined here without consulting the menu.

White Shutters on Peachtree   683 Peachtree St. N.E., Tel.
873-7721
  Good home-cooked foods served pleasantly, also home-baked
  pastries.

24-Hour Restaurants

Kafe Kobenhavn   Regency Hyatt House, 265 Peachtree St.
N.E., Tel. 577-1234
  This is a sidewalk café in the courtyard of the hotel, where
  you can watch the world come in.

The Fairfield Inn   Marriott Motor Hotel, 165 Courtland St.
N.W., Tel. 688-6500
  Whether you want a man-sized meal or a cup of soup at 3
  A.M., the Fairfielders are always cheerful and willing.

*The Midnight Sun restaurant, designed and decorated by
Atlanta architect John Portman, offers Danish specialties. Located beneath the Gas Light Tower plaza*

Night Life

THOUGH WE blush to admit it, you can find whatever you want in Atlanta night life.

We have topless girls, girls with tails, girls without tails, revolving spotlights, deafening sound, stomping, thudding, drilling and enough general uproar to pulverize the nervous system.

We have promoters, wheelers, dealers, exotics, eccentrics, funny people; bland-eyed bachelors with briefcases; girls who transcribe by day and transmute by night, and thousands of new conventioneers every week with husbands, wives or companions, all away from home, one way or another.

It was like this, really, from the beginning. Atlanta wasn't settled by cavaliers. Trappers, traders, tie-tussling men aren't likely to settle for minuets and musicales for their fun.

One of the really great openings of the year 1875 was the inauguration of a splendid, gaudy saloon on Decatur Street, replete with French mirrors, frescoes, white marble counters and a bar of solid silver. It was called the Big Bonanza.

Apparently Atlanta has always had a considerable thirst.

It tried prohibition one time on its own, but it failed. On May 19, 1933, when the Volstead Act was repealed, 49 establishments had been licensed to sell beer by nightfall. A few were selling while the city fathers debated an ordinance. "We can't even get it cold," said one harassed bartender. "They drink it up almost as fast as we put it on ice."

So, since only you know what you are looking for, here is a list of Atlanta-on-the-rocks night spots, rendezvous, joints, happenings and places. Prices and cover charges will be your own concern. It's like owning a yacht; if you have to ask the price, you'd better be sure you do.

Before the crowd closes in, we do recommend:

Wit's End   50 Fifth St. N.W., Tel. 875-5405.
> More the beginning of wit than the end. The cleverest original satire east or west of the Mississippi; where New York and Hollywood comedy writers drop in for ideas. Showtimes Mon.–Thurs., 10 P.M.; Fri., Sat., 10:30 and 11:30 P.M.

Atlanta Dinner Theater (Southwest)   2939 Campbellton Rd. S.W., Tel. 349-2277
> Dinner from 7 to 8 P.M. Legitimate theater from 8:30, nightly except Sunday.

Tally Ho Dinner Theater (Sandy Springs)   6521 Roswell Rd. N.E., Tel. 252-3820
> Dinner from 6:30 to 8:30, 6 nights weekly. No Mondays. Curtain at 8:30 with plays changing frequently.

More Lounges and Supper Clubs

Falcon Restaurant and Lounge   774 W. Peachtree St. N.W., Tel. 874-2252
> Top-flight entertainment of the Las Vegas variety. Dinner from 4 P.M. to midnight, mainly choice steak. Open Mon.–Sat. until 2 P.M.

The Lion's Head   1915 Peachtree Rd. N.E., Tel. 355-7130
> Mon.–Sat., 11:30 A.M. for lunch through 2 A.M.

Top of Kitten's Korner   845 Peachtree St. N.E., Tel. 875-8357
> Lunch 11:30; dinner from 6:30 P.M.; supper 11:30 P.M–2:30 A.M. Very live entertainment.

Jennings Supper Club   931 Monroe Dr. N.E., Tel. 875-8901
Luncheon from 11:30 A.M., cocktails 4 P.M., dinner 7 P.M.–
midnight. Dancing to big-name bands.

The Brave-Falcon Lounge and Restaurant   2329 Cheshire
Bridge Rd. N.E., Tel. 636-4868
Live-wire entertainment, steaks, sandwiches, 4 P.M.–2 A.M.,
except Sundays.

Ruby Red's Warehouse   51 Old Alabama St. (Underground
Atlanta), Tel. 524-9748
Banjo-strummin', rowdy music, fun and games, from 7:30
P.M. week nights, 9 P.M. weekends. No Sundays.

The Playboy Club of Atlanta   Inn Town Motor Hotel, 89 Luckie
St. N.W., Tel. 525-4626
Entertainment nightly with floor show, jazz groups. Open
11:30 A.M.–2 A.M. Saturdays from 5 P.M. Breakfast served
after midnight.

Tally-Ho Lounge   Yohannan's Across the Street, 3393 Lenox
Rd. N.E., Tel. 261-3491
Dining, dancing, cocktail hour; open 11:30 A.M.–1 A.M. for
breakfast, lunch, dinner.

The Habersham Room   Yohannan's Lenox Square, Tel. 233-
1191
Dancing, supper shows at 9:30 and 11:15 P.M. Open Tues.–
Sat., 8 A.M.–12:30 A.M.

The Blue Cockatoo   4420 Roswell Rd. N.W., Tel. 252-3464
Lunch 11 A.M.–2 P.M.; dinner 7–10 P.M. Live entertainment
beginning at 4 P.M. Dancing until 2 A.M.

Carrousel Inn   Yohannan's Lenox Square, Tel. 233-1191.
Paneled, red-velvet 90s atmosphere. 11:30 A.M.–1 P.M. No
Sundays.

Club Atlantis   Regency Hyatt House, 265 Peachtree St. N.E.,
Tel. 577-1234.
Headline entertainers begin performances at 9 P.M., con-
tinue until 2 A.M. Mon.–Sat., 11:30 A.M.–2 A.M.

The Scene   114½ Ponce de Leon Ave. N.E., Tel. 873-2603.
A discotheque for young swingers. Mon.–Sat., 8 P.M.–2 A.M.

Whisk'-a-Go-Go   355 Peachtree St. N.E., Tel. 523-7909.
This place helped start the discotheque era. Mon.–Sat., 5
P.M.–2 A.M.

The Roaring Sixties   2581 Piedmont Rd. N.E., Tel. 261-3175.
Food and fun. Mon.–Sat., 5 P.M.–2 A.M.

The Playroom   1006 Peachtree St. N.E., Tel. 892-8669.
Country Western's home in Atlanta. Entertainment from 9
P.M. Mon.–Sat. Open 5 P.M.–2 A.M.

The Red Dog Saloon   3106 Peachtree Rd. N.E., Tel. 237-6831.
Back to Bonanza days, with all the Western atmosphere.
Piano nightly, jazz sessions Saturday afternoons. Open 11
A.M.–midnight.

The Windjammer Lounge   Marriott Motor Hotel, 165 Courtland St. N.W., Tel. 688-6500
Buffet lunch 11:30 A.M.–2:30 P.M.; cocktails, dancing every
night except Sunday. Sat., 5 P.M.–2 A.M.

There are many more big frenetic spots and discreet
cool ones.

Finding your own laughing place might be part of your
discovery of Atlanta.

Wit's End Players, Nancy and Phil Erickson, present clever satire
on any and all subjects.

Four Tours of Metro Atlanta

Tour 1

SPEND THE first day downtown, getting your bearings.
You might like to divide the ambitious walking tour de-
scribed on page 23 into two parts, punctuating the sorties
by lunch.

Now we'll concentrate on the next four days.

Downtown Atlanta has no grand design. In the beginning, few people thought there would be a town here at all,
so every man built on his land just to suit himself. There
are no mitered corners on this patchwork map.

The city is divided into quadrants. Everything is marked
N.W., N.E., S.E., and S.W.

We'll go Northwest first, where the city's imposing
residences dominate the landscaped greenswards and
where history, past and present, sets the mood.

The journey will not be as the crow flies. The route may
be as the creek runs or the winds blow or even as the
Cherokee Indians soft-moccasined a hundred or more

ORIENT YOURSELF UPTOWN

(1) Life of Georgia Building

(2) Fox Theatre

(3) Citizens and Southern National Bank, North Ave. branch

(4) The Varsity Drive-In

(5) The Sheraton-Biltmore Hotel

(6) St. Mark's Methodist Church

(7) North Avenue Presbyterian Church

(8) First Baptist Church

(9) Lutheran Church of the Redeemer

(10) St. Luke's Episcopal Church

(11) Grant Field

(12) Georgia Institute of Technology tower and campus

(13) New Coca Cola Building

(14) The Doctors' Building

(15) Crawford W. Long Memorial Hospital

(16) Atlanta Memorial Arts Center

(17) Entrance to Piedmont Park

(18) Alexander Memorial Coliseum

years ago before they marched off on their last sad Trail of Tears.

Take Peachtree North. Your first points of interest will be at North Avenue and Spring Street with an aggregation of architectural exclamation points. The beautiful white marble Life of Georgia building dominates the commercial cluster. Close to it the 16-story cylindrical bronze anodized aluminum tower of the Citizens and Southern Branch Bank stands like a massive sculpture.

This is Atlanta's Uptown section.

The North Avenue Presbyterian Church, First National Bank's North Avenue branch, a high-rise apartment called Peachtree North, the 11-story Ivey Building and the redoubtable Varsity drive-in restaurant are all within three or four blocks.

The Varsity is the world's largest drive-in eatery. If you make this scene about noon, you may be trampled by people heading there for a hamburger or a hot dog. You may want to join the crowd because Varsity food is good. This whole enterprise is a real success story for the proprietor, W. Frank Gordy.

Beyond this, still on North Avenue, is Coca-Cola's new 12-story expansion with its auditorium. This is Coke's home and international headquarters. Speaking of success stories, this one is shared by practically every millionaire in Atlanta.

And we never overlook the Life of Georgia millionaires either. Rankin Smith, owner of the Atlanta Falcons football team, is one of the owners of this thriving institution.

To your left at this point is the *Georgia Institute of Technology*, better known as Georgia Tech. When Tech opened in 1888 with 85 students, it had room to grow. Now the school is an island in an urban area.

Tech is going west. It has developed a plan, with the help of Atlanta's urban renewal program, for the use of 60 additional acres surrounding its historic tower. By 1985 it will have transformed the community around it.

You may not want to detour to visit Tech, because parking is a problem on its campus, but if you do, special points

Tower of Georgia Institute of Technology is historic landmark on downtown campus.

of interest are the Nuclear Reactor on Atlanta Avenue and the Price Gilbert Memorial Library with its seven-story addition for graduate work; the latter has the largest collection of technical books in the South.

At Peachtree and Ponce de Leon, on your right, is the Georgian Terrace Hotel, an architectural gem. This is where the stars used to stay when the Metropolitan Opera came splendidly to the Fox Theater, across the street. The Cox-Carlton, a family-owned hotel, is its seemly neighbor.

The huge *First Baptist Church* at 754 Peachtree N.E. is also nearby, as are St. Mark's Methodist and the Lutheran Church of the Redeemer and, within several blocks, All

Atlanta Memorial Arts Center sends forth glow at night from its illuminated peristyle on Peachtree Street.

Saints Episcopal at 634 West Peachtree N.W., First Methodist at 360 Peachtree N.E., and St. Luke's Episcopal at 435 Peachtree N.E., the latter two having served large congregations for a hundred years or so.

Crossing Peachtree is the Tenth Street shopping area, faintly reminiscent of Greenwich Village with its art-movie houses, coffeehouses, art galleries and street flower vendors. It leads toward the focal point of this community, the *Atlanta Memorial Arts Center,* between 15th and 16th streets on Peachtree.

The Memorial Arts Center is the newest pride of Atlanta. It opened in the fall of 1968, a $13 million or more memorial to the 122 men and women art patrons who died in an air crash in Paris in 1962 at the end of a summer holiday. The Center, operated by the Atlanta Arts Alliance, embraces all the visual and performing arts.

Across the street from the Memorial Center is Colony Square, a $40 million complex of office buildings, a hotel, two houses, high-rise apartments, restaurants and shops in the process of development.

You're going to drive out Peachtree as far as Buckhead.

You'll go through territory that only a few years ago was exclusively residential and now has given way to booming commerce.

Notice the bronze markers along the way indicating points of historical interest. Most of them mark sites of fierce Civil War battles. Don't wander off on Peachtree Memorial, Peachtree Circle, Peachtree Way, Peachtree Battle or any of the other Peachtree derivatives.

You'll go past Pershing Point, where West Peachtree melds into Peachtree; past the Jewish Community Center, ornamented with mosaics by Perli Telzig, Israeli sculptor; past the black Peachtree-Palisades Building, which rises with great flair at 1819 Peachtree Road; through the Brookwood area with its English village façades.

The Peachtree-Palisades Building poses behind Elbert Weinberg's bronze statue of Eve in immortal struggle with the serpent. The building has added drama inside. Seven artists—Joe Almyda, Lamar Dodd, Ferdinand Warren, Ed Ross, Maxine Yalovitz, Joel Reeves and George Beattie—have spotlighted each of the building's seven floors with paintings of their own choice.

A mile or so farther north, after you cross Peachtree Creek, is *Peachtree Battle*, which earned its name. In this area, the Bobby Jones Golf Course and the Bitsy Grant Tennis Center, both public facilities, are off to the left on Northside Drive. You won't see them on this route, but you should know they were named for two of the city's athletic Hall of Famers.

Up the road, where Andrews Drive points back into Peachtree Road, the *Cathedral of St. Philip* (Episcopal) rises in considerable grandeur on a point known informally as Holy Hill. Across from St. Philip's are the *Cathedral of Christ the King* (Roman Catholic) and the *Second Ponce de Leon Baptist Church*. They create a genteel traffic jam on Sundays and all religious holidays.

You will know you are in Buckhead when you reach another five-pointed intersection.

Though you won't see them on this trip, beyond to the north are Oglethorpe University, Chastain Memorial Park, Peachtree Golf Club and the Peachtree Industrial Boulevard, where dozens of major national manufacturers have their regional plants, as well as the country preserve of the Capital City Club.

Also to the north are Lenox Square and its haute-shopping companion, Phipps Plaza. They're both out Peachtree Road, a mile or two north of Buckhead. Lenox was Atlanta's first regional shopping center and is still its most impressive. Phipps is a complex devoted to high fashion retail and quality service stores, one of the newest in Atlanta. It is billed as "Fifth Avenue on Peachtree."

Buckhead is more than a point. It is a point of view. Around Buckhead in all directions are elegant homes with columns, acreage, atriums, Georgian façades, pools, poodles and yard men. Not gardeners, please. They're indispensable enough, already.

We would like to have you turn left at West Paces Ferry but you can't. There's a No Left Turn sign there, as we go to press. Take the second tentacle of the starfish intersection, go a block and turn back until you sidle into West Paces Ferry heading west. That's the crucial street at this point.

Drive right to Andrews Drive, turn left again and within a block or so you will see, rising grandly on your left, Swan House.

Be sure to visit *Swan House*. It's the home of the Atlanta Historical Society, the Walter McElreath Memorial.

You are directed to Swan House for many reasons. It is the epitome of old and proud Atlanta. Its grounds are a microcosm of the gentle sloping, the magnificent trees, the native shrubs, the wild flowers, the fresh air and sheer beauty that has been the extra ingredient in Atlanta's appeal.

The furnishings of Swan House are celebrated for value and suitability. No mere restoration, this was the home of the late Edward Inmans, in use and glowing with the patina of perfection when the property was acquired in 1967.

In addition to a museum of Atlantiana, including a gallery of photographs of Atlanta from its first days until the

Swan House, home of the Atlanta Historical Society

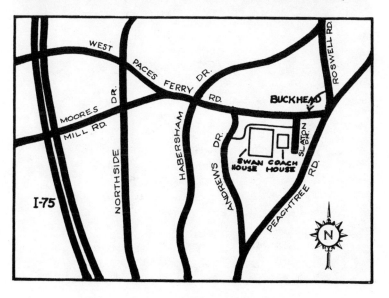

The Coach House of Atlanta Historical Society features good food and art objects for sale.

The Governor's Mansion stands in Greek splendor, an island in an ocean of trees on West Paces Ferry Road N.W.

present, there are other archives and the Margaret Mitchell Memorial Library. Miss Mitchell's father, Eugene Mitchell, was one of the founders of the Atlanta Historical Society, and her family has continued his interest.

Swan House and its gardens were designed by Atlanta architect Philip Trammett Schutze, inspired by the Palladian school of architecture. Many of its panels and doors were carved in England. There are swan motifs in several places, notably in the important Chippendale swan consoles and in the capitals of the Corinthian columns in the great dining room. In the rear of Swan House is the Coach House, a restaurant, art gallery and gift shop made from a renovation of the original servants' quarters. It is run by the Forward Arts Foundation, a group of Atlanta women interested in promoting the enjoyment of visual arts. You may lunch here by telephoning 261-0636 for reservations.

If you stay for lunch, save room for a pastry from the cart.

As you drive away, notice the entrance to the Cherokee Town and Country Club just across the street as you move out West Paces Ferry headed west. This was the old Grant estate, which has been made into one of the city's most impressive private clubs.

Still going west, you will see the $2 million *Governor's Mansion*, a red-brick structure in the Greek Revival spirit, the cynosure of all eyes since it opened in 1968. It is the third Governor's Mansion since the capital was removed to Atlanta from Milledgeville.

The official home, named the Executive Center, was designed by A. Thomas Bradbury in the columned symmetry beloved in the South. It was furnished, decorated and landscaped under the supervision of a Fine Arts Committee, headed by Henry Green of Madison, Georgia.

With its Federal American furniture of the 1785–1835 period and its English pieces, marble mantels, Aubusson and Savonnerie rugs, porcelains, draperies, and fine American paintings, Executive Center has already become Atlanta's museum of the decorative arts.

*Bulloch Hall was the Roswell, Georgia, home of Mittie (Martha)
Bulloch, who married Theodore Roosevelt, Sr., here in 1853.*

It is open to the public daily (except Saturday) from 10
A.M. until late afternoon.

West Paces Ferry has many beautiful homes. You will
pass Pace Academy, the erstwhile Ogden residence, another of the manorial houses copied exactly from a European original.

Turn north at the intersection of West Paces Ferry and
U.S. 41. But before you do, you will want to know that
beyond the intersection to the left are the Westminster
School for Boys and Girls, a fine grouping of neo-Colonial
structures, and the Lovett Schools, equally new, in contemporary style. These are Atlanta's leading private pre-
paratory schools.

U.S. 41, which is also known as the Northwest Expressway extension, cuts through as impressive a landscape as
any you will find on the Piedmont plateau. Try not to get
tangled up and end up on I-75.

Cross the Chattahoochee River and pass both *Lockheed*

Aircraft Corporation's huge facility and Dobbins Air Force Base.

Lockheed, which came to Georgia in the early 1950s, turns out the C-5 Galaxy, the largest cargo plane in the world. With 25,000 employees, Lockheed is Georgia's largest employer.

Dobbins Air Base was named for Captain Charles Dobbins of Marietta, a pilot who lost his life in World War II. Now, with the Naval Air Station, which uses its runways, it is the largest Air Reserve training center in the world. The host unit is the 44th military (Dixie) Airlift wing. There are ten tenant units based within its compound.

Drive beyond Dobbins to the intersection of Highway 120, turn right and go to Roswell. *Roswell* is a picturesque town cherished in Georgia for the felicity of its early residential architecture and its role in the Civil War.

It was founded in 1835 by comfortably well off families from Savannah and Darien who wished to escape the malarial torpor of summer in their coastal areas. Their notable residences still stand and are in private use. You may glimpse Mimosa and Bulloch Halls, the Goulding Place, the Archibald Smith House, Great Oaks and Allenbrook, all of which are visited as reverently as Virginians turn to Monticello. Stately Barrington Hall is open to the public during the summer months, when Miss Evelyn Simpson, the owner, will welcome you.

Bulloch Hall was the home of Miss Martha Bulloch, who married Theodore Roosevelt. Their son, Teddy, returned as President to greet old family servants and receive a hero's welcome from all Roswell.

Not far from here is the scene of the Shakerag Hunt, where Atlanta's sporting gentry bound to the hounds over beautiful and spacious lands. It is also the scene of the annual Greater Atlanta Steeplechase, a springtime event that brings riders, mounts, spectators and fans from everywhere to respond to its starter's bugles.

You may want to dine at *Lickskillet Farm Restaurant* on Old Roswell Road, which you will find by following signs or asking directions in Roswell. Lickskillet is an orderly, flavorful and surprising rural restaurant open for dinner every evening except Sunday from 6:30 until 11:30, offerign a citified menu of prime ribs, lobster, etc., preceded by hot hors d'oeuvres, homemade soup, and morsels of hot hoecake. It is complete with bar, soft piano and wood fires crackling in season. Occasionally, when the mood is upon its two gentlemen proprietors, the establishment may serve a "country" supper. The country menu wil provide such old-time delectables as hickory-cured ham and sausage seasoned to its own recipe, baked yams, grits, hot apple sauce, baking-powder biscuits, sweet butter and such.

It would be wise to call 475-6484 for reservations.

If you find it is too late to include the Roswell tangent on this junket, return to Atlanta on U.S. 41 and watch for the Smyrna signs on the right. Have dinner at *Aunt Fanny's Cabin,* if it is getting along toward that hour.

Aunt Fanny's is a caution. It is a ramshackle old slave cabin with numerous afterthoughts in the form of dining lean-tos, quaint and successful with its manners and menu of the old Hallelujah South. Thousands of guests, including most of the nation's food editors and magazine writers, bursting with fried chicken and brotherly love, have penned their tributes to its South-Will-Rise-Again cuisine.

If you dine at Aunt Fanny's ask them to point you back toward U.S. 41 and drive south. It will take you back downtown.

If you are not exhausted, telephone *Wit's End.* See if Phil and Nancy Erickson and their chums have a show on the boards. They play in season and only on certain nights in their own club. You may be served a drink or so while you watch the performance. The Ericksons are old playmates and professional colleagues of Dick Van Dyke. Their original satires do for Atlanta, in reverse, what the Historical Society does in the affirmative.

By now you may be ready for some irreverent spoofing. The Ericksons and company do it best.

Today, why not try a Northeast passage? The big things to see in this section are *Fernbank Science Center* and *Stone Mountain,* that unbelievable old heap of granite. There's plenty more, but either of these could command the day.

Drive out Piedmont Avenue. You will go past Atlanta's gala new Civic Center. It is less than two years old and is already being enlarged.

When you cross Ponce de Leon, you will know that the street was named from a fountain of youth. Early settlers found delight and, they hoped, more abundant health in the waters of a spring in this community. Old Ponce de Leon Springs flourished for a while as a favorite resort.

Out Ponce de Leon, about two miles to your right, is the regional headquarters of the Presbyterian Church U.S. for the Southeast. A lot of other things are out Ponce de Leon too, including the prosperous city called *Decatur.*

Since you'll be going past *Piedmont Park,* detour slightly to the right and meander through Atlanta's largest public playground. Piedmont Park has had many lives, including being the site of 19th century fairs and a course for trotting horses. Now, among other things, it is the setting for the week-long Atlanta Arts Festival frolic each May.

The Atlanta Arts Festival is a sensory celebration with exhibitions, paintings, sculpture, crafts, photography, industrial design, drama, symphonies, chorales, pantomine, folk singers, jazz, ballet, modern dancing—a joyous rite of spring which involves hundreds of men, women and children.

If the season is right, some fine horticultural specimens may be seen in Piedmont's flower house.

The trees are a glory at any time. Horse chestnuts bloom in the spring and gingko trees are hung with tiny golden fans in the autumn.

A small Japanese bonsai garden is tucked near the

greenhouses in this park. Its stepping stones, pools, bamboo, stunted pines, dwarfed plants and one perfect black locust centered around a tiny teahouse are all the work of the Atlanta Bonsai Society, directed by Felton E. Jones.

Piedmont Park also has a fragrance garden for the special delectation of persons with impaired vision.

Lovers are always in season here. A city ordinance permits them to pause and hold hands or kiss discreetly without inviting arrest.

In an enclave of this park is the city's most exclusive private play place, the *Piedmont Driving Club*. This is where the really gala balls are held and where Atlanta's most assured belles have been presented to society since the Cotton States Exposition in Piedmont Park made the 1890s in Atlanta very gay indeed.

Stay on Piedmont until it crosses East Rock Springs Road to the right. East Rock Springs will take you to the *Emory University* neighborhood. Emory is Atlanta's great private university.

In this area are four major hospitals and the burgeoning national headquarters of the United States Department of Public Health's Communicable Disease Center, all clustering around Emory's outstanding School of Medicine.

Also in this area are some of the most pleasant homes and gardens in Atlanta. In April, when the dogwoods are in full bloom, the Lullwater Road section is incredibly lovely.

Turn off East Rock Springs Road onto Clifton Road and drive close to *Fernbank Science Center*. It will be at your left at 156 Heaton Park Drive.

Fernbank is new, the third largest planetarium in the United States, with an electron-microscope laboratory and an observatory housing a 36-inch telescope, one of the most powerful in the Southeast. The 60-acre virgin forest, a conservation area, with carpets of moss, wild flowers and fern-bordered streams, is open for botany studies.

Fernbank was the home of Miss Emily Harrison, whose

Fernbank Science Center in Druid Hills section

family cherished the forest for its natural growth and animal life. Miss Harrison, a schoolteacher for more than 50 years, planted many of the Fernbank trees herself as a child.

The observatory, which is operated as a teaching facility by the DeKalb County School system, is open to the public from 8 until 11 P.M. Wednesday and Friday nights, when nights are clear. Scientific exhibits are on display from 8:30 A.M. to 9 P.M. weekdays, until 5 P.M. on Saturdays, and from 2 to 5 P.M. on Sundays. The forest itself is open from 2 to 5 P.M. on weekdays and Sundays. There is an admission charge of $1.00 for non-educators. It might be wise to check times by telephoning 378-4311.

You are not far from *Agnes Scott College*, Decatur's excellent fine arts college for women, and the Columbia Theological Seminary owned by the Presbyterian Synods of

Georgia, South Carolina, Alabama and Mississippi.

When you leave Fernbank, stay on Clifton Road and drive left until you come to Ponce de Leon Avenue. Go left on Ponce de Leon to its confluence with U.S. 78. Right on 78 will take you to *Stone Mountain,* which was once called New Gibraltar for obvious reasons. It is one of Georgia's, and the world's, natural wonders.

If you are interested in lunch, stop at the *Plantation House Restaurant.* It's on U.S. 78, about two miles before you get to the mountain. Try the family-style dinner. Family style means gourmand platters of chicken and meats, heaped-up serving dishes of vegetables, such extras as grits and red-eye gravy (don't knock it until you've tried it), crackling bread, biscuits and suitably fattening desserts.

Drive on to Stone Mountain for the afternoon. Take the skylift cable car to the 730-foot crest of this igneous intrusion. During the five-minute ascent you will see clearly the world's largest sculpture of equestrian figures, as high as a nine-story building.

This carving of Confederacy President Jefferson Davis and Generals Robert E. Lee and Stonewall Jackson has had its troubles. In the mid-20s the United Daughters of the Confederacy had plans to carve this gigantic memorial but money ran out and disagreements set in. Sculptor Gutzon Borglum did not finish the memorial. Sculptor Walker Hancock is now at work on it. If you think it is not impressive, consider that Mr. Borglum entertained 40 guests at breakfast in his time on the shoulder of General Lee and nobody fell off.

But other people have been falling off Stone Mountain since time immemorial, most of them school youngsters on gravity-defying and dangerous larks. The mountain looks like a half-submerged whale, but it has its steep side, too. Old Mountain hero Elias Nour himself had been credited with saving 37 or 38 lives when he retired a few years ago.

When you get to the top of the mountain, you can see practically forever. Your view will have a 90-mile radius, stretching in all directions over cities, towns, forests, fields, lakes and highways. If you don't experience a little awe and pleasure at this moment, you've wasted your time at Stone Mountain.

There are picnic places, reflecting pools, Confederate flags waving in the breeze, and models of the monumental sculpture up there, but the most astonishing thing is the clarity of the air, the stunning vista and the trees and shrubs that have pressed up inexorably from the apparently soilless granite.

Incidentally, at least three very rare horticultural specimens may be found atop the mountain. The yellow Confederate daisy, *Vigiera porteri*, blooms in September. Stone Mountain's St. John's Wort, the *Hypericum splendens*, is found sparingly and thrusts out its rusty red blossoms in June. The *Phacelia maculata*, blue-spotted scorpion weed, blooms in May.

Stone Mountain itself is the climax of this adventure, but there are other things that should be done. You can't miss the scenic railroad with its five-mile run around the base of the mountain, complete with Indian ambush and suitable war whoops. Children, old and young are properly terrified. You'll ride the paddleboat *Robert E. Lee*, hear a 610-bell carillon, see a moonshine still and a sorghum mill.

You may buy some of the sorghum (but no moonshine) at the Country Store, which is part of the antebellum plantation complex. The plantation is the best thing at Stone Mountain Park, next to the awesome rock itself. It gives everybody a new insight into why the rebels thought the way of life in the Old South was worth dying for.

The plantation complex is both restoration and reproduction. The eleven buildings, including the Big House (which is neither white nor columned), the overseer's house, slave cabins, the "necessary" house, cookhouse and gazebo, were brought from various points in Georgia and reconstituted here. Their carefully authenticated furnishings are all appropriate to the period at the turn of the 18th century.

The plantation's old smokehouse is used to cure hams

Skylift rises above carving of Confederate Memorial at Stone Mountain. General Robert E. Lee is central figure.

Steamboat General Robert E. Lee *paddlewheels along lake at Stone Mountain Park in front of monolith.*

for the Country Store. The kitchen gardens grow herbs and spices, as well as summer vegetables for its counters. In addition to these, the Country Store sells such things as sourwood honey, slabs of hickory-cured bacon, water-ground cornmeal and sunbonnets—in case you are subject to the vapors.

You must see the *Thornton House*. For 180 years this little house stood, as snug as a little wren in its buff-washed squareness, at Union Point, Georgia, surrounded by a white picket fence enclosing the boxwoods, the vegetable and flower gardens, the herbs and the orchards of pear and apple trees.

The house was then moved to Atlanta to the grounds of the Atlanta Art Association to be put on display as an example of garden planning, architecture, furnishings and

Magnolia Hall is central building in re-creation of Old South Plantation complex at Stone Mountain. Photo below shows Kingston House, the overseer's home.

the decorative tastes of a generation of pioneers. It gave moderns a real-life view of social history.

To make way for the Memorial Center on Peachtree Street, Thornton House has been moved once again. This time it has come to rest at Stone Mountain Memorial Park, where it has become a part of the reconstituted plantation group.

This will have been a rugged, ozone-spiked day, so take the straightest road back to Atlanta and your hotel.

Go left on U.S. 78, which becomes Memorial Drive as you approach town. Stay on it. It will take you within sight of the glittery dome of the Capitol. You can find your way back to base from there.

This might be a fine night for dinner at *Justine's* on Piedmont Road. Justine's is elegant in a shiny-parquet, polished-silver, aristocratic way.

If you can't absorb any more Old South, try *Gene and Gabe's* little Italian restaurant on Piedmont Avenue. Their antipasto is piquant, their veal succulently pink.

Tour 3

Unless you are a researcher of the past, or unless you have children who can stare for hours at exotic and familiar animals, this probably will be only a half-day jaunt.

Without intending undue sentimentality, your first gesture today might be *Oakland Cemetery*. Oakland, the city's oldest burial place, was established in 1850, and was virtually sold out at the turn of the 20th century. Confederate soldiers, paupers, generals, senators, governors, slaves, millionaires comprise the more than 100,000 persons whose names appear on ornate mausoleums or weatherbeaten stones. Among them is Margaret Mitchell, who had a novelist-historian's special regard for Oakland and its silent memories.

You will reach Oakland by driving east on Mitchell Street until it becomes Memorial Drive. A few blocks out Memorial

Atlanta's oldest cemetery, Oakland, where Margaret Mitchell is buried. This view shows Confederate Memorial.

Drive on your left is Oakland with its 85 acres, its stillness surrounded by a brick wall.

You are on hallowed ground here. Many battles were fought in this area, which is not far from Fort Walker in Grant Park.

Fort Walker, atop the hill near the Atlanta Avenue and Boulevard entrance to Grant Park, was held by a Confederate battery during the Battle of Atlanta in 1864. The hill was named in memory of William H. T. Walker, Confederate general, who was killed in that battle.

Fort Walker is a camera buff's delight, a spectacular view of the skyline framed by a Civil War cannon in the foreground.

Grant Park has all the usual accouterments of a city park, but the principal attractions are the Zoo and the Cyclorama.

The *Cyclorama* is an astonishingly vivid three-dimensional pictorial person-to-person evocation of all the battles of the bloodiest of American wars. This circular painting was completed in 1886 by a group of German artists in Milwaukee. It celebrates the crucial moment at 4:30 P.M., July 22, 1864, when "Abe," the eagle mascot of Union Company C soared high above the exploding shells, charging soldiers and the rising smoke of the battlefields.

The guide at the Cyclorama will give you more information in printed pamphlets, and a tape-recorded voice will fill you in with details of the panorama. A lecture is given on the half hour. There is a small charge.

In the basement of the Cyclorama building stands "The Texas." "The Texas" is an old Western and Atlantic railroad steam engine which on April 11, 1862, won an audacious victory. Running backwards, it chased and caught the line's engine "The General," between Adairsville (Georgia), and Chattanooga when "The General" was seized in a daring "kidnaping" by 22 Federal spies under James J.

Scene from the Cyclorama, remarkable painting in the round depicting the Battle of Atlanta, 1864

Guanaco mother displays her baby at Grant Park open-air zoo.

Andrews. The story of the Andrews Raiders and the two steam engines was the subject of a movie "The Great Locomotive Chase."

Now stroll over and visit the big happy families at *Grant Park Zoo.* The Zoo, directed by John Roth, is the most impressive wild-animal community in the Southeast, with everything from three-toed sloths to elephants domiciled in as-close-as-possible replicas of their natural habitat.

The zoo has recently completed a $5 million improvement program, including a new reptile house where such residents as a green mamba slither menacingly through the foliage behind glass.

Madelyn, the tiger, and Gus, the leopard, roar and snarl in a symphony with the lions and the lesser cats in the feline house, which, with the primate house, the bear lair and the sea-lion circus, draw thousands of men, women and children every day.

The Children's Zoo is a special place. Every day by early light, children and their parents find their way here to touch the velvety ears of the baby burro or gingerly poke at a sprouty-haired infant elephant. The Children's Zoo has a toy train chugging around, and a merry-go-round, one of the few carrousels using hand-carved zoo animals for mounts. It's a gay, antique delight and a continuing trap for young parents who learn from Grant Park's merry-go-round that their child has fallen hopelessly in love for the first time with a painted ostrich or a laughing pig.

One of the features of the Zoo's Primate House is the Raiford Ragsdale Science Teaching Television Room, from which programs are beamed to classrooms through the network of the Atlanta public school system. In addition to solar systems, geological materials and many other exhibits, live snakes peer out from glass cases and small animals are regularly brought to the room to be televised. In the spring, when many baby animals are born, schoolchildren are taken on a television tour of the whole zoo.

This general geographical area is in the center of Atlanta's 3,000-acre Model Cities program, which will be in progress for several years as all of the social and welfare sources of the city are brought into effective application.

You are not far from the *Southeastern Fair Grounds*. You can take Boulevard South to McDonough; then jog west on McDonough to Sawtell Road, which will lead you to Lakewood and South Bend Parks and the Fair Grounds.

Lakewood operates an amusement center from May through October with carnival atmosphere and facilities. October is the month of the Southeastern Fair. At the close of the autumn fair season, Lakewood Park is also closed.

Administration Building of the State Farmers' Market

As you go toward the Fair Grounds, you will cross Jonesboro Road. Jonesboro is the refugee road down which terrified Atlanta families streamed in 1864, fleeing from the burning of their homes toward a settlement called "Rough and Ready."

On your way south on Jonesboro Road or Interstate 75–85, you will be near Georgia's new Farmers Market in Forest Park. It would be a good place to stop for a vegetable lunch or a watermelon feast. Aside from its gustatory attractions, it is a fascinating exchange for products from the farmlands of Georgia and the gardens and groves of the world.

When you leave Grant Park you are only a short distance from Confederate Avenue, site of the New Georgia State Police Academy, State Patrol Headquarters, Georgia National Guard and the former site of the Confederate Soldiers' Home. This home was recently demolished. The last frail widows of Confederate soldiers linger at a rest home in Atlanta, the guests of the state.

You are not far from the United States Penitentiary, which you will not be likely to visit unless you are a relative of a prisoner or have business to transact. The Penitentiary has been open since 1902. It was designed to shelter 2,000 inmates, most of them adult serious offenders. Al Capone was one of many malodorous celebrities who slept here.

If you are going to *Lake Spivey,* one of the ways to get there is via the Jonesboro Road. Follow it as far as the town of *Jonesboro.* Signs will tell you when to turn for Spivey's three beaches. Perhaps an easier way would be to get back on Interstate 75 and drive south until you see the Jonesboro Exit sign.

There is an interesting Japanese restaurant, *Sada Yoshi-*

One of Lake Spivey's beaches south of Atlanta

numa's, on Highway 41, near Jonesboro. You might try it for luncheon.

Lake Spivey is an 1800-acre spring-fed lake developed within the last ten years by Dr. and Mrs. Walter Spivey for a family holiday and vacation place. No alcoholic beverages or pets are allowed. There is a mile of white sand beach, 250 acres reserved for fishing, sailing, speedboating and practically all water sports, a playland for children, a fort, Indian villages, daily Western shows in the summertime, picnic grounds, refreshment centers and several moderately priced buffets and cafeterias.

Lake Spivey is open from the last weekend in April through Labor Day. However, it has a public campsite, with all conveniences for camping and trailering, which stays open until later in the season. For specific information call 478-8861 or write Lake Spivey, Route 1, Jonesboro, Ga.

In the peach season, you will notice signs for do-it-yourself peach picking in neighboring orchards. Try it. Tree-ripened peaches will make you an addict for life.

This is the end of the line for today. Head back to Atlanta on Interstate 75-85.

You'll go right past the Stadium. If the place is alight, you may want to round out your exhaustion with an evening ball game.

The Atlanta Braves have *not* been here since the Civil War. They came in 1966.

Tour 4

Todays itinerary will introduce you to the most important center in the world for Negro education. You may also see some of the fine residences occupied by prosperous Atlanta Negro business and professional men and their families.

This aspect of the city illustrates in part the communication and understanding that have existed over the years between the white and Negro communities of Atlanta.

Straight west on Hunter Street will take you to *Atlanta*

University, a complex of six associated Negro colleges which were established within 15 to 20 years after the Civil War.

Atlanta University is the center for graduate and professional courses in Education, Social Work, Library Service, Business Administration and Arts and Sciences. It was established in a box car in 1867 by representatives of the American Missionary Association.

Associated with Atlanta University are Clark, Spelman, Morris Brown and Morehouse Colleges and Gammon Theological Seminary.

Dr. Rufus Clement, late President of Atlanta University, was the first Negro member of the Atlanta Board of Education.

Down the street from the University Center on Hunter and C Streets is the Booker T. Washington High School, with a monument to its famous namesake shown in a group of bronze figures at its main entrance.

Not far from here, a little to the south and west, at 1050 Gordon Street S.W., is the *Wren's Nest,* a chirpy little Victorian cottage which was the home of Joel Chandler Harris while he was writing and publishing his *Tales of Uncle Remus.*

Within the house are displays of autographed letters, pictures, personal possessions and original editions of Harris' works. Outside it, is a walk made of pink Georgia marble, each section inscribed with the name of a writer and author.

This area of Atlanta is known as West End, the birthplace of many of the city's leaders through the turn of the 20th century. West End is now undergoing a considerable face-lifting under urban renewal planning.

To the south on U.S. 20 is *Fort McPherson,* headquarters of the Third Army. Fort Mac is the home of one of five continental armies, the largest in number, men and activities. Seven southeastern states are within the Third Army's jurisdiction, nine forts, 225,000 military and 30,000 civilian personnel. Fort Mac itself has 4,000 personnel.

Just before you get to Fort McPherson, take Campbellton Road to the right if you wish to visit *Greenbriar,* the South's largest shopping center under one roof. Greenbriar is made up of many shops and stores and is the focal point for this growing urban radius.

If you'd like to lunch at Greenbriar, try Happy Herman's Sidewalk Cafe, where the pizza is special.

If the Perimeter road (under construction as this goes to press) has been opened, follow your map to get back to 285, north to its intersection with L-20, which will lead you directly to Atlanta's answer to Disneyland, Six Flags Over Georgia.

Six Flags over Georgia (Spain, France, Great Britain, Colonial, Confederate and Federal) is the state's most concentrated playtime attraction, a mammoth American-type Tivoli Gardens.

The Wren's Nest, home of Joel Chandler Harris, where the Uncle Remus stories were written

Entrance to Six Flags Over Georgia on Atlanta's I-20 West

Train ride takes one on circumferential tour of Six Flags.

Trained porpoises delight Six Flags onlookers.

It opened in 1967 as a 75-acre amusement area and in one short season it entertained 1,110,000 people. Immediately its owners embarked on an expansion program.

Six Flags represents an outlay of more than $15 million by the Great Southwest Corporation.

One ticket ($4.50 for adults, $3.50 for children) opens the turnstile to 75 rides and amusements, excluding the food emporia, of course. Jaded visitors who do not respond to flying saucers or visits to true-to-life gold mines and such will be refreshed by the design of the buildings and pleased with the landscaping. They will also appreciate the fresh-faced and mannerly young people who make up the park's staff.

The park opens on April 13 for weekends. On June 1, it opens for seven days a week. After Labor Day it is open only on weekends once more, for as long as the weather permits.

Parking is ample and convenient, and you won't go hungry. Each Flag offers a typical cuisine. There are also benches for sitting and watching the world go by.

Botanical specimens and fine sculpture provide visual delights at Six Flags.

Special Annual Events

I F Y O U C A N stay awhile, we suggest that you scan this list of special annual events to see what's likely to be going on.

Specific dates of the events listed below shift every year. Check the Sports and Amusements sections of the Atlanta newspapers, especially the Sunday edition, for specific details, but here is the general calendar of perennial pleasures:

JANUARY: General Assembly opens second Monday for six weeks. Passes for the Legislature may be obtained from the Speaker's office; for the Senate from the Lieutenant Governor's office.

FEBRUARY: Atlanta Boat Show, Exhibition Hall, Civic Center.
Camellia Show, usually at Auditorium, Lenox Square.
College Southeastern Conference Basketball Tournament, Tech Coliseum.

MARCH: Atlanta Constitution-Georgia High School Association, state-wide Class AAA basketball tournament at Tech Coliseum.
State Class AA Basketball Champion, G.H.S.A.A., Tech Coliseum.

	Atlanta Braves pre-season baseball game, Stadium.
APRIL:	Atlanta 500, International NASCAR Race, International Raceway, Hampton, Ga.
	Atlanta Hunt Meeting and Steeplechase, Seven Branches Farm, just off Holcomb Bridge Road, Roswell.
	Dogwood Festival (no place as beautiful as Atlanta with 200,000 dogwoods in full flower). Concerts, fashion shows, music, lighted trails, floodlighted trees, sports—sponsored by the Chamber of Commerce of Atlanta Women.
	Opening of Chiefs' Soccer Season, Stadium.
	Opening of Braves' Baseball Season, Stadium.
	Shrine Indoor Circus, Old Municipal Auditorium.
	Tulip Festival, Hurt Park.
	Tour of Homes, sponsored by Henrietta Egleston Hospital.
	Masters Golf Tournament, Augusta.
MAY:	Metropolitan Opera Week, Civic Center.
	Atlanta Arts Festival, Piedmont Park.
	Stone Mountain All-Arabian Horse Show, Stone Mountain.
	Armed Forces Day, Lockheed plant.
	Atlanta Classic Golf Tournament, Atlanta Country Club.
JUNE:	Jazz Festival, Stadium.
	Greater Atlanta Horse Show, Chastain Park.
JULY:	Watermelon Day, Farmers Market.
	Atlanta Sports Festival July Jubilee, ten-day sports and entertainment spectacular leading up to July 4, with baseball, soccer, tennis, water sports, softball, Masters parachute jump, and WSB-TV's gala Fourth of July Parade.
	World's Fair for Youth, 10 days, Atlanta Civic Center.
AUGUST:	Atlanta Falcons, pre-season game, Atlanta Stadium.
SEPTEMBER:	Fashionata, Rich's two-day fashion extravaganza and revue, Marriott Motor Hotel.
	Greater Atlanta Arts Congress, usually at Regency Hyatt Hotel.
	Opening of Falcons' Football Season, Atlanta Stadium.

Special Annual Events   111

Opening of Georgia Tech's Football Season, Grant Field at Tech.

Opening of High School Football Season.

OCTOBER: Southeastern Fair, Lakewood Park. An overflowing cornucopia of products, people, progress and play.

Cracker Crumble, Georgia Press Association's Journalistic Inquisition, usually at Marriott Motor Hotel.

Atlanta Hawks, pre-season game, Tech Coliseum.

NOVEMBER: Lighting of Great Tree, Rich's, Thanksgiving Night.

Georgia Tech Freshmen—Georgia University Freshman Charity Football Game, Grant Field, Thanksgiving afternoon, for benefit of Scottish Rite Children's Hospital.

"Heaven Bound," performance at Big Bethel Baptist Church, Auburn Avenue.

Christmas Trees Around the World, Cherokee Garden Club, Lenox Square Auditorium.

DECEMBER: *Nutcracker Suite,* Atlanta Ballet, Atlanta Pops Orchestra, Atlanta Choral Guild, several performances during holiday fortnight in Memorial Arts Center.

Peach Bowl Game (college football teams), Grant Field at Tech.

Arts Festival in Piedmont Park displays art in its myriad forms.

Sports

If it's a game, somebody is playing it in Atlanta.

The city is a fired-up, hoarse-voiced crowd of 1,300,000 sporting spectators and peerless participants huddled at the epicenter of 3,000,000 more superfans within an hour or two's reach of the junction of three interstate highways.

With National Football League Falcons, National League Braves, North American Soccer League's Chiefs and National Basketball Association Hawks, Atlanta is the professional sports capital of the South. There are golf, tennis, bowling, hunting and trap shooting; fishing, camping, sailing, yachting, steeplechasing and horse racing; sportscar rallying, sky diving, parachute jumping, sail planing; water and mountain skiing, every type of ball game, roller and ice skating, swimming, scuba diving and dozens of other muscle-flexing pursuits. We even have a group of falconers so keen on King Arthur's sport that they are experts at gluing fresh tailfeathers on their pet peregrines.

The city that in 1930 welcomed home the incomparable Robert Tyre Jones, Jr., from his Grand Slam in golf with a frenzied parade, is hard to one-up in golf. Three hundred caddies carried aloft signs that bespoke the sentiment of

Atlanta Stadium during night game of the Atlanta Braves. The Falcons and the Chiefs play here also.

Atlanta Falcons in action at the Stadium

the entire crowd then and now: WELCOME BACK, MR. BOB, YOU SHO' BROUGHT BACK THE BACON!

After Bobby Jones came Alexa Stirling, Charlie Yates (British Amateur Champion in 1938), Dorothy Kirby and Louise Suggs.

Fans have been yelling "Play ball!" in Atlanta since 1864, when the first home-run ball of the season covered a quarter of a mile, presumably downhill, and was not recovered for two weeks. Final score: 127 to 29.

Before the Braves' currently amazing Henry Aaron and Felipe Alou, there were such men as Ty Cobb and Napoleon Rucker.

Tug and Pull was the popular formation in football in the rugged '90s, when no player was out until he called himself down. In the interim years there have been such legendary groups as Georgia Tech's Golden Tornados, the great Indian Joe Guyon, Red Barron and Everett Strupper, as well as dozens of indomitable grid performers developed under the leadership of coaches Bobby Dodd of Tech and Wallace Butts and Vince Dooley of the University of Georgia.

Now Atlanta has its own bowl classic, the Peach Bowl, which was inaugurated in 1968 at Grant Field.

The Falcons play a full professional season at the $18

million Atlanta Stadium, the Yellow Jackets of Georgia Tech draw 52,000 fans to Grant Field every time they run on the field, and every high school and prep school in the state is hysterical with football fever.

If the Atlanta Braves aren't warming up in the bullpen at 521 Capital Avenue S.W., the Atlanta Chiefs may have a soccer game at the Stadium, or the Hawks may be lobbing in baskets at Alexander Memorial Coliseum.

If none of this is happening, don't forget the NASCARS roaring at the International Raceway on the South Expressway (U.S. 41), 25 miles due south of Atlanta. The Atlanta International presents three international racing events a year, which bring drivers and fans—as many as 80,000 each time from everywhere—clogging roads for two days before and after each event. In 1968 Bobby Allison set a track record of four laps at 155.805 miles per hour in his Ford.

Dragsters scratch off at the National Hot Rod Association-sanctioned Southeastern International Dragway at Dallas, Georgia, 30 minutes to the northwest of Atlanta.

Midgets skid around the Peach Bowl Speedway at 1040 Brady Avenue N.W.

Specifically, there are 28 golf courses in metro Atlanta. Fourteen are private clubs, seven are public, and eight commercial.

The Georgia Tech's Ramblin' 'Reck leads the Yellow Jackets on to Grant Field.

The Atlanta Classic Golf Tournament commands late May at the Atlanta Country Club. The Atlanta City Open, for pros as well as amateurs, is held here each May. In August, Druid Hills Club is the scene of the Atlanta City Amateur for men.

Atlanta hosts the Junior Masculine Tournament, the Girls Junior, the Atlanta Women's Amateur, the Atlanta Womens' handicap and, periodically, the State Amateur Championship matches for men and women.

Basketball takes over in the winter. The Coliseum seats 7,000 and it is practically always sold out for Tech's college games. It is also the aerie of the professional Hawks. When neither of these teams is using the courts, state high school tournaments rouse great partisanship at the prep age level.

There are roughly 175 tennis courts in the five-county area of metro Atlanta, the most outstanding of which is named for Bryan (Bitsy) Grant, who won the U.S. Clay Court Championship in 1930 and is still a formidable opponent.

More than 200 separate bowling leagues for men and women, and dozens of mixed and teen-age leagues, are sanctioned by national bowling associations. There are as

WHERE TO PLAY

1. American Legion G.C., Albany
2. Adams Park G.C., Atlanta
3. Bobby Jones Municipal G.C., Atlanta
4. Candler Park G.C., Atlanta
5. College Park G.C., College Park
6. East Lake #2 G.C., Atlanta
7. North Fulton G.C., Atlanta
8. Piedmont Park G.C., Atlanta
9. John A. White, G.C., Atlanta
10. Augusta G.C., Augusta
11. Green Meadows C.C., Augusta
12. Midland Valley C.C., Augusta
13. Lithia Springs G.C., Austell
14. Barnesville G.C., Barnesville
15. Appling County C.C., Baxley
16. Blairsville G.C., Blairsville
17. Mapleleaf G.C., Bremen
18. Brunswick C.C., Brunswick
19. Cairo C.C., Cairo
20. Calhoun Elks Club, Calhoun
21. Royal 200 G.C., Chatsworth
22. Evans Heights G.C., Claxton
23. Skitt Mountain G. & C.C., Cleveland
24. Nebo G.C., Dallas

25. Dawson G.C., Dawson
26. Piedmont College G.C., Demorest
27. Douglas C.C., Douglas
28. Dublin C.C., Dublin
29. Dodge County G.C., Eastman
30. Pineknoll G.C., Eatonton
31. Folkston G. & C.C., Folkston
32. Chattahoochee G.C., Gainesville
33. Sand Greens, Glennville
34. Griffin Municipal G.C., Griffin
35. Legion G.C., Hartwell
36. Town & Creek C.C., Hawkinsville
37. Jeff Davis G.C., Haxlehurst
38. Hogansville G.C., Hogansville
39. Jekyll Island Championship, Jekyll Island
40. Pine Lakes G.C., Jekyll Island
41. Oceanside G.C., Jekyll Island Golfing privileges at courses 39, 40, and 41 for guests of Buccaneer Motel, Corsair, Jekyll Estate, Stuckey's Carriage Inn and Wanderer Inn.
42. Jessup G.C., Jessup

43. Lakeshore C.C., Jonesbor
44. Riverside G.C., Jonesbor
45. Municipal G.C., LaFayett
46. Highland C.C., LaGrange
47. Walker G.C., Lawrenceville
48. Linvalley C.C., Lindale
49. Mystery Valley G.C., Li nia
50. Louisville G.C. Louisville
51. Little Ocmulgee State P G.C., McRae
52. Bowden G.C., Macon
53. Par 56 G.C., Marietta
54. Monroe G. & C.C., Monro
55. McKenzie Memorial G Montezuma
56. Pinecrest C.C., Pelham
57. Airport G.C., Callaway Gardens
58. Lakeview G.C., Callawa Gardens
59. Mountain View G.C., laway Gardens
60. Quitman C.C., Quitman
61. Reynolds G.C., Reynolds
62. Goodyear G.C., Rockma
63. Collier Springs G.C., R
64. Hard Labor Creek State P Rutledge
65. St. Mary's G.C., St. Mar

A golfers' map of Georgia

66. **Sea Palms G. & C.C., St. Simons Island**
   Golfing privileges for guests of King and Prince Hotel and Sailfish Motel, St. Simons Island; The Cloister, Sea Island; Holiday Inn and Oak Park Motel, Brunswick.
67. **Bacon Park G.C., Savannah**
68. **Mary Calder G.C., Savannah**
69. **Savannah Inn & C.C., Savannah**
70. **Windsor Forest G.C., Savannah**
71. **Plantation G.C., Sea Island**
72. **Retreat G.C., Sea Island**
73. **Sea Side G.C., Sea Island**

Golfing privileges at courses 71, 72 and 73 for guests of The Cloister.
74. **Brown Bell G.C., Senoia**
75. **Briar Creek C.C., Sylvania**
76. **Twin City G.C., Tennille**
77. **Belle Meade C.C., Thomson**
78. **Thomson C.C., Thomson**
79. **Glen Arven C.C., Thomasville**
80. **Greene County C.C., Union Point**
81. **Sandy Run G.C., Warner Robins**
82. **Washington-Wilkes C.C., Washington**
83. **Waynesboro C.C., Waynesboro**
84. **Jug Tavern G.C., Winder**

many more playing outside leagues. In May of each year, Atlanta's Carling Brewing Company sponsors the Carling Open Bowling tournament, bringing in top national professionals. Atlanta is the home of Wayne Zahn, top pro bowler in the country.

The metro area has almost 5,000 acres of public parks. Atlanta itself has 48 major parks, four of them downtown, with, at the moment, 125 small parks and greenways, whose number is being increased constantly under a program of coordinated school-park development.

In these parks there are extensive recreation programs. There are approximately 500 baseball and softball diamonds and 500 football fields, 37 recreation centers, 57 playgrounds and seven public golf courses. They are geared to serve everyone from kindergarten children to people of post-retirement age. The City of Atlanta's recreation division entertains at least three million participants each year in its swimming pools, health clubs, music, dancing, crafts and seasonal sports programs.

With vast and beautiful lakes to port and starboard— Lanier, Allatoona, Burton, Rabun, Hartwell, Jackson, Sinclair, Seminole and Clarks Hill—Atlanta is the inland-water capital of the world.

There are something like 315,860 acres of lakes, 4,000 miles of shoreline, dozens of yacht and sailing clubs and innumerable houseboat and lakeside homes within an hour or two of Atlanta. Lakes Sidney Lanier and Allatoona, both about 50 minutes from the city, attract at least 11,000,000 visitors between them during the year.

The city has a long lease with the U.S. Corps of Engineers for a 476-acre tract of land on the north shore of Lake Allatoona, where beach and boat ramps, campsites, day camping facilities have already been established, and riding trails, athletic fields, a crafts center and marksmanship ranges are in development.

There are more than 30 public recreation areas at Lake

Allatoona, and Lake Lanier, three times as large, with its 540-mile shoreline, has its quota of public facilities.

Three flotillas of the U.S. Coast Guard Auxiliary, volunteer men and women banded together as the civilian arm of the Coast Guard, run a Sundown Patrol at these two lakes during the summer months to offer assistance to those who need a tow, are lost, or have engine trouble.

Boats failing to return at expected hours are provided with a Search and Resecure service operated on a volunteer basis. (Note: Resecure—not rescue.)

Fishing is a passion in Georgia. The state is crisscrossed with a network of 17 rivers which are fed by 3,000 miles of tributaries and 700 miles of mountain streams. In addition to its vast reservoir system, Georgia has 40,000 small lakes and ponds and a saltwater coastline of approximately 1,000 miles.

A hundred and twenty-four species of fish have been catalogued, 32 of which are excellent game fish. Some of the best trout fishing spots are found in wildlife management areas in the Chattahoochee National Forest to the north of Atlanta.

On the Atlantic Coast, rivers, creeks and sounds wind into 520,000 acres of estuaries and marshes between coastal islands and the mainlands. Fish are found everywhere the water goes—speckled trout, mackerel, redfish, king.

Lake Seminole, at the confluence of the Flint and Chattahoochee rivers, which form the Appalachicola, is the most outstanding fishing reservoir in the southeast.

A call at the Georgia Parks Department, 7 Hunter Street S.W., or the Georgia Fish and Game Commission, 401 State Capitol, or the U.S. Corps of Engineers, 30 Pryor Street S.W., will elicit all additional information.

Don't forget hunting. Within 100 miles of Atlanta are 500,000 acres of public hunting areas in the Chattahoochee National Forest along Georgia's northern border, where

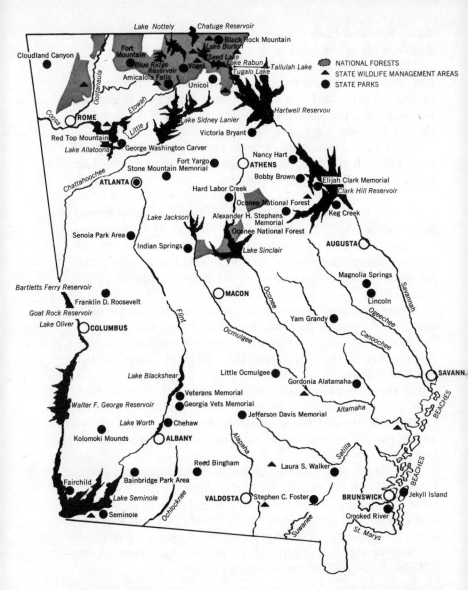

Fishing map of Georgia invites you to wet a hook in the state's many lakes and streams, or deep-sea fish off the coast. Catch may be rainbow, brook, or brown trout; white, striped, largemouth, smallmouth, spotted or redeye bass; channel catfish, walleye, chain pickerel, black or white crappie; yellow perch, warmouth, redbreast sunfish or bluegill.

quail, rabbit, racoon, 'possum, squirrel, dove and deer are to be found.

Deer may be hunted in 85 of Georgia's 159 counties. The Virginia Whitetail roams the coastal swamps of south Georgians. Nonresident visitors also will find fees relatively a recent year, north Georgia yielded about half the 13,000 deer killed in the entire state.

Fishing licenses cost $1.25, hunting licenses $2.25 for Georgians. Nonresident visitors also will find fees relatively inexpensive: $10.25 for small game and $20.25 for both large and small game.

In the spring, there are enough tents on any given day in Georgia's mountains and along its streams in summer and fall to rehouse the entire erstwhile Indian population. More than 70 developed camping sites exist in state parks and along the shores of its reservoir lakes, as well as on its public lands in the forest to the north.

The Recreational Department of Atlanta organized the Metropolitan Atlanta Family Camping Association a few years ago. It meets monthly to discuss camping problems and plan camping expeditions.

With the ski jumps of Tennessee only a few hours away, Atlanta's Ski Club is the second largest in the nation.

There are seven ski areas in North Carolina and Tennessee, within a 300-mile radius of Atlanta, with more developing all the time. Cattaloochee ski slopes above Maggie Valley in North Carolina, Gatlinburg ski resort in the Tennessee Smokies, Blowing Rock Ski Lodge and Hound Ears Lodge at Blowing Rock in the Blue Ridge Mountains, High Meadows, Beech Mountain and Sapphire Valley resorts, all serve as local Zermatts or Innsbrucks, offering all facilities for skiing and other winter sports. Each resort has both beginner slopes and expert trails, with indoor and outdoor ice skating as a sideline feature in several.

Track conditioning never stops in Atlanta.

One must drive carefully down any quiet street. There is always someone clad in sweatshirt and trunks, jogging on the sidewalk or to one side of the pavement getting in shape for a school track meet—or it may be a bond salesman out for his morning's sprint. Informal running is the big thing in body building. All the runners need is an Olympic torch.

A local attorney tells of his morning run around the block in which he is joined by his game and agile wife. "We have finally started holding hands as we run," Hamilton Lokey says. "Until we did that, everybody thought Muriel was chasing me."

Ticket Information

ATLANTA BRAVES:

Atlanta Stadium, 9 A.M. to 5 P.M., Saturdays 9 to 1 P.M. When season starts, advance ticket window open until 9 P.M. daily
Downtown Ticket Office, Broad and Marietta Sts., 9 A.M. to 5 P.M., 9 to 12 noon Saturdays
Other agencies: Davison's (Downtown, Lenox Square and Columbia Mall stores); Ellers News Stand, Forest Park; Western Union, Cobb County Chamber of Commerce
Groups of 15 or more: Delta and Southern Airlines
Via mail: Atlanta Braves, P.O. Box 4064, Atlanta, Ga. 30302
Season: Opens in April; pre-season game in late March

ATLANTA CHIEFS:

Atlanta Stadium, 9 A.M. to 5 P.M., Saturdays, 9 to 1 P.M.
Downtown Ticket Office, Broad and Marietta Sts., 9 A.M. to 5 P.M., 9 to 12 noon Saturdays
Other Agencies: Western Union, Delta and Southern Airlines, Davison's Downtown, Lenox and Columbia Mall
Season: Opens in April

ATLANTA FALCONS:

Atlanta Stadium, 9 A.M. to 5 P.M., Saturdays 9 to 1 P.M.
Advance Ticket Window, Gate G, 9 A.M. to 5 P.M.

Via mail: Atlanta Falcons Ticket Office, Atlanta Stadium, Atlanta, Ga. 30312
Season: Opens in September; pre-season game in late August

ATLANTA HAWKS:

Alexander Memorial Coliseum, I-75-85 North Expressway at 10th St.
Tickets: Tel. 688-4600
   Write Atlanta Hawks, 148 Cain Street N.E., Atlanta, Ga. 30303
Other agencies: Davison's Downtown, Lenox and Columbia Mall

ATLANTA INTERNATIONAL RACEWAYS:

Write Hampton, Ga.
Tel. 946-4211

Atlanta's International Raceway shown during famous annual Atlanta 500

The Arts

Theater

WITH FOUR legitimate show houses and still another projected for the near future, the curtain is always going up in Atlanta on classics and original scripts, experimentals, comedies, absurdities.

The plush new 868-seat Alliance Theater in the Atlanta Memorial Arts Center, 1280 Peachtree Street N.E., is the home of both the Atlanta Childrens Theater and the Alliance Resident Company.

The Academy Theater, 3312 Roswell Road, performs original and experimental plays along with other serious works, including an occasional season of Shakespeare. Its Academy Childrens Theater has a special series.

The Community Playhouse, 1150 Peachtree Street N. E., invites smaller productions, and the Atlanta Civic Center with 4,560 seats in its Robert Maddox Hall is the setting for performances of visiting musicales and dramatic productions.

Theater Atlanta, the city's oldest dramatic group, left its handsome theatrical home at 1374 West Peachtree Street

N. E. in early 1969 to take its own production of *Red, White and Maddox* to Broadway.

Another legitimate showhouse, a penthouse seating 2,000, has been designed as part of the Peachtree Center complex. When it is opened, it will present all-professional Broadway companies.

Two major impresario agencies have had a long history in Atlanta.

Famous Artists Corporation, 952 Peachtree Street N.E., is the oldest booking agency in the United States. Mr. and Mrs. Ralph Bridges book concerts, Broadway musicals, exhibition games, teen-age rock-and-roll groups, orchestras and other performances for 22 cities in the Southeast. Their most tumultuous presentation in recent years was the Beatles, who drew 34,000 screaming fans in 1966 to the Atlanta Stadium.

J. Lee Friedman, manager of the Atlanta Music Club's several series, is another successful Atlanta impresario; he has brought "Holiday on Ice" to Atlanta for 23 years, as well as other national companies of musical productions. Mr. Friedman also produces with Radio Station WPLO three shows a year in the country-western field called "Shower of Stars."

All the colleges perform theatrical works. The Emory Players, Georgia Tech's Drama Tech, the Players at Georgia State, the Oglethorpe Players and Agnes Scott's Blackfriars have full seasons on their campuses.

Baldwin W. Burroughs of Spelman College presents the Atlanta-Morehouse-Spelman Players in a six-week summer season at Atlanta University.

Several dinner theaters, serving food and drama, play to full houses in both meanings of the word.

Ticket Information

Academy Theater   3212 Roswell Rd. N.E., Tel. 233-9481
Academy Childrens Theater   3212 Roswell Rd. N.E., Tel. 233-9481

Alliance Resident Theater 1280 Peachtree St. N.E., Tel. 524-3845
Atlanta Childrens Theater 1280 Peachtree St. N.E., Tel. 876-6843
Atlanta Civic Center Theater Box Office, 395 Piedmont Ave. N.E., Tel. 523-1879
The Barn Dinner Theater Terrell Mill Road, off Marietta Highway No. 41, Tel. 436-6262
Community Playhouse 1150 Peachtree St. N.E., Tel. 872-9177
Tally Ho Dinner Theater 6521 Roswell Rd. N.E., Tel. 252-3820

NOTE: Tickets for most of these performances may also be obtained at Davison's ticket counter on the mezzanine floor, downtown store, or at Rich's downtown store. Many may be charged to accounts. A call to above numbers will direct you to other ticket counters.

Community Theater Groups

College Park Little Theater Tel. 761-0710
River Theater Tel. 255-3887
Southwest Community Theater Tel. 344-2678
Stageplayers Tel. 767-7361

Movies

Growth patterns have made Atlanta one of the best movie cities in the country.

Commuters have an exasperating time pressing homeward through the afternoon rush, but getting back downtown when the traffic has given up is another matter. With radial expressways fingering out in all directions, moviegoers can make it back downtown a mile a minute at movie time.

And they do. Atlanta has a perennial appetite for movies. The city has been the star, of course, in two of the great ones: "The Birth of a Nation" and "Gone With the Wind." Both panicked the populace.

The first premiere of "Gone With the Wind" was as much a spectacle on the streets and in the ballrooms as it was on the screen. Its most recent premiere, in 1967, brought out more panoply and excitement, white ties, evening gowns and speechmaking to Margaret Mitchell Square in front of Loew's Grand Theater.

Atlanta's Fox Theatre, with its star-twinkling clouds floating overhead, known far and wide as the Fabulous Fox, is the second-largest movie house in the United States.

At the other end of the spectrum is George Ellis's suave Festival Cinema at 142 Spring Street N.W., with 95 gently rocking seats (no popcorn, but Viennese coffee with whipped cream), which shows art films to suit Ellis's own sophisticated tastes.

Atlanta's first-run theaters are:

Capri Cinema
   3110 Roswell Rd. N.W.
   Tel. 233-3361
Cherokee Theater
   3861 Peachtree Rd. N.E.
   Tel. 237-6517
Coronet Theater
   630 Peachtree St. N.E.
   Tel. 874-8935
Fox Theater
   660 Peachtree St. N.E.
   Tel. 872-8866
Lenox Square Theater
   Lenox Shopping Center
   Tel. 233-0338
Loew's Grand Theater
   157 Peachtree St. N.E.
   Tel. 688-6696
Martin's Cinerama Theater
   583 Peachtree St. N.E.
   Tel. 875-9405

Martin's Georgia Cinerama Theater
   2210 N. Druid Hills Rd. N.E.
   Tel. 634-1266
Martin's Rialto Theater
   34 Forsyth St. N.W.
   Tel. 525-5661
Rhodes Theater
   11-A Rhodes Center N.W.
   Tel. 876-7919
Roxy Theater
   204 Peachtree St. N.E.
   Tel. 688-5133
Tara Theater
   LaVista & Cheshire Bridge Rds.
   Tel. 634-6288
Theatre Atlanta, Inc.
   1374 W. Peachtree N.E.
   Tel. 892-8000

Music

In May, when Atlanta cannot contain the jubilation of spring, when every dogwood petal is a suspended snowflake, every azalea and tulip bursting with life, the Metropolitan Opera comes to the city.

It is as if the city had found its voice and that voice were limitless, pure and powerful and perfect beyond hope.

Atlanta has had a love affair with the Met, off and on, since 1910.

But grand opera is not the indigenous music of Atlanta.

The persimmon pucker of a country boy's ballad, the simplicities of sacred harp, cotton field laments, spirituals, hot rock, soul, cool jazz, stomps, blues, moans, hallelujah work songs, chanties, legends, confessions—these are the natural expressions of our people.

Music is one of the arts about which the city is not even a teeny bit self-conscious. Perhaps the only one.

Many people deserve credit for this: Irish immigrants laying rails, remembering the greenness of another land; Scots tussling timbers for railroad ties, the skirl of bagpipes echoing in their ears; mountain folks from the Appalachians plucking their lilting dulcimers; early Negroes with their vocal supplications.

The heroines of fine music in Atlanta are the indomitable matrons who for 53 years have made up the Atlanta Music Club. They have scolded, wheedled, persuaded and prayed for support. Because of them, Atlanta has heard every artist of stature since World War I.

The years have brought them all: Sergei Rachmaninoff, Artur Rubinstein, the Menuhins, Fritz Kreisler, Kirsten Flagstad, Marian Anderson, Pablo Casals and many more.

The Atlanta Symphony was one of the babies of the Atlanta Music Club. Through hard-pressed years, with Henry Sopkin as the valiant maestro, it grew to become one of the nation's major symphony orchestras. Now under the baton of the celebrated Robert Shaw, the 89-piece Atlanta Symphony plays a full season of 100 concerts in five separate series, presenting distinguished soloists and visiting conductors in its opulent new 1,848-seat concert hall in the Memorial Center.

Atlanta's Choral Guild of 275 voices (another of the Atlanta Music Club's fringe benefits) has been in existence since 1939. Under the direction of Don Robinson, it dedi-

Rehearsal time in Symphony Hall in Memorial Arts Center, where Robert Shaw conducts the Atlanta Symphony Orchestra.

cates itself to performances of choral literature not available from other musical sources.

The Atlanta Boys Choir, directed by Fletcher Wolfe, is an exquisite success.

Mr. Wolfe is also musical director of the Atlanta Chamber Opera Society, Inc., which produces major chamber operas each season, using local and regional talent and, occasionally, singers of established national reputation.

William M. Lemonds, head of Emory University's music department, directs the 80-member Emory Glee Club in 60 or more performances over the South, the Emory Woman's Chorale with 90 voices and the Emory Chamber Singers. He organized and directs the Atlanta Chamber Orchestra at Emory with a complement of 48 members, and between times travels as visiting conductor and baritone soloist.

Georgia Tech's outstanding Glee Club presents regular

concerts annually at the Fox Theatre and makes periodic concert tours elsewhere in the nation and in Europe.

Tech's 100-piece band performs smartly at football games and in appearances at public functions, as well as on the high school circuit.

The state has its own official band, the Concert Band of Georgia, with 30 members, draws musicians from 75 miles away. It is directed by Anthony Bel Castro.

The Pro-Mozart Society, promulgated by Mrs. Robert Bunzl, wife of the Austrian Consul, presents artists in concerts of Mozart's works each winter season. These appearances are scheduled for the Walter Hill Auditorium in the Memorial Center.

Dance bands, combos, folk-singing groups are here by the dozens.

Bill Clarke, called "the Pied Piper for a generation," is Atlanta's answer to Lester Lanin. He has played for debutante parties and college functions since 1937.

The Sorta Forties, a combo of business men, former professional musicians of the age indicated in their name, are great swingers.

For specific musical events, check the Atlanta newspapers, especially the Sunday sections dealing with music and the arts.

Tickets are usually available to everything but the Metropolitan Opera performances.

If you hear of any of those floating around, let us know!

Ballet

Ballet and dance perform great pas de deux in Atlanta.

The Atlanta Ballet, with Robert Barnett and Carl Ratcliff as Director and Associate Director, is a full-fledged repertory company. Its principal performances are staged in the Alliance Theater of the Atlanta Memorial Arts Center, 1280 Peachtree Street N.E.

The Atlanta Ballet, founded in 1929 by Dorothy Alexander, is the oldest regional company in the nation. In addition to its professional corps, it has a regional troupe which serves as a training corps for the professional company. It also has a junior company.

One of the highlights of the Christmas season is the Atlanta Ballet's gala performance of Tschaikovsky's "Nutcracker Suite" in its entirety. This performance also combines the talents of the Atlanta Pops Orchestra and the Atlanta Choral Guild.

The Southern Ballet of Atlanta, which presents a spring season of programs, is headed by Pittman Corry and Karen Conrad. It was organized in 1945 and now includes junior, intermediate and senior troupes. Lottie Hentschel is a third director.

The Atlanta Concert Dance Group, headed by Ruth Mitchell Kimbrell, performs excitingly in the jazz, contemporary and classical forms, often inviting guest choreographers for special performances. Productions are usually staged in the Community Playhouse, 1150 Peachtree Street N.E.

Two other ballet companies are active in the metro area. Decatur-DeKalb Civic Ballet, directed by Hilda Gumm and Marie Roberts, was founded in 1953 as a junior company of the Atlanta Ballet. It now operates independently.

Iris Antley Hensley, one of the lead dancers of the Atlanta Concert Dance Group, founded the Marietta School of Ballet and Marietta Civic Ballet in 1957, the first ballet company in Cobb County's history.

Tickets for performances of these companies may be obtained at the following places:

Atlanta Ballet
 1222 Peachtree St. N.E.
 Tel. 892-0638

Atlanta Concert Dance Group
 3509 Northside Parkway N.W.
 Tel. 237-8829

The Southern Ballet
 ½ West Paces Ferry N.W.
 Tel. 233-5831

Decatur-DeKalb Civic Ballet
 102 Church St., Decatur
 Tel. 378-3388

Marietta Civic Ballet
 322 Cherokee St., Marietta
 Tel. 428-6356

If you have nine daughters in a row, name them for the muses and send them to Atlanta. They'll have a good home with a Peachtree address.

But don't expect them to live happily ever after.

Art is here, all over the place, in studios, basements, schools, pads. It is volatile, explosive, defiant, sometimes tentative and anxious. Fortunately, it is never boring.

Which, of course, is what art is all about—an eternal search to express the inexpressible.

This yeasty climate of discontent, leavened with need, acceptance and mutual blessing, has been with us since 1926, when the late Mrs. J. M. High bequeathed her Peachtree home to the city and asked that it be known as the High Museum of Art.

It polarizes now in a great new temple between 15th and 16th streets on Peachtree known as the Atlanta Memorial Arts Center.

The Memorial Center is a veritable United Nations of the Arts, embracing the High Museum of Art, the Atlanta Symphony, the Atlanta Childrens Theater, the Alliance Resident Theater Company, the Atlanta School of Art, the Walter Hill Auditorium, a library, several galleries and other components.

The building materialized out of public response to an airplane crash at Orly Field in Paris in 1962 that took the lives of many Atlantans and Georgians returning from a pilgrimage to the artistic monuments of Europe.

The initial sympathy tokens, small in themselves, engendered an anonymous gift of $7 million from an Atlanta philanthropist, which was met by an additional $6 million from public contributions.

The J. J. Haverty family of Atlanta led the first movement in 1905 toward establishing the first art association and the city's first art school.

The Atlanta School of Art is now a four-year school,

granting a degree, with facilities for 300 students, occupying an entire floor of the Memorial Center.

Joel Reeves, himself a notable artist, heads the school, which is a member of the University of Georgia Center.

Gifts for the High Museum have come from many sources throughout the years. The excellent collection of the Haverty family forms its artistic nucleus.

Mrs. Thomas K. Glenn, the Henry B. Scott Fund and Mrs. Ralph K. Uhry are responsible for significant gifts. The Uhry collection includes lithographs, etchings, engravings and woodcuts by Munch, Toulouse-Lautrec, Picasso, Matisse, Kandinsky, Renoir, Degas, Marin and Baskin.

Keystone of the High Museum's collection is the Samuel H. Kress gift of 30 Italian Renaissance paintings, a rare prize worth $3 million, given in 1953. Among the Kress treasures are a Bellini, a Tintoretto, eight Lorenzo Costa panels of saints, and a wood sculpture of the 15th-century German artist Tilman Riemenschneider.

The most evocative art object at the Center may be its newest major acquisition, Auguste Rodin's heroic mourning figure "L'Ombre" (the Shade), the gift in 1968 of the Republic of France.

The new Rodin figure joined other important bronzes at the Center. Virginio Ferrare's "Tragic Flight" was another commemorative gift, made by hotel magnate Albert Pick, Jr., and Mrs. Pick of Chicago.

Throughout the years many notable artists have come to lecture and act as guest instructors at High Museum. The Museum's collection also includes examples of their works. Among them are Yasuo Kuniyoshi, Frederic Taubes, Carl Gross and Dong Kingman.

The museum has a representative collection of contemporary paintings including works by Alexander Brook, George Grosz, Zoltan Sepeshy, Josef Albers, Stanley Hayter, Adolph Gottlieb, Allen Jones, Eduardo Paolozzi, Gabor Peterdi, Georges Rouault, Karl Schmidt-Rottluff, Felix Vallotten and Victor Vasarely.

Recently acquired paintings include works of Joseph Perrin, Lloyd McNeill, Ben Smith, Gladene Tucker, Floyd Coleman, Ida Kohlmeyer, Jarvin Parks, Charles Demuth and Richard Anuskiewicz.

Since classical works of distinction are in short supply and the competition for them is tremendous, Atlanta's High Museum, along with other small museums throughout the world, will concentrate on 20th-century art in its future major acquisitions.

The art mix is kept rich by colleges.

On its downtown campus, Georgia State College's new Fine Arts Building, a $3 million structure front-yarding on Hurt Park, with its own galleries and small music hall, will soon open.

Joseph Perrin heads the School of Art, which offers three professional degrees in the visual arts and includes courses in photography and cinematography in its curriculum.

At Agnes Scott College, Ferdinand Warren heads the Arts Department with studios and galleries in the new Dana Fine Arts Building.

The coordinated Arts Department of the Atlanta University group in headed by John D. Hatch, Jr.

Atlanta University possesses the largest collection of paintings, drawings, sculpture and prints by Negro artists in America, including some recently acquired pieces of African art. These superb works, as well as traveling collections, are on exhibit at the Catherine Hughes Waddell Gallery.

One of the high points of the year in art is the veteran Southeastern Art Competition, initiated in 1945 and now under the sponsorship of Davison's, the Atlanta Junior League and the National Bank of Georgia, in cooperation with High Museum of Art.

At least 1,000 entries from artists through the Southeast and elsewhere are considered for awards by professional judges.

Another cultural stimulus is the Spring Arts Festival,

which flings paintings, sculpture and every kind of art expression into a village-green array in Piedmont Park each May. More than 200,000 persons stroll through the Festival each spring.

The graphic arts are recognized with two other major competitions, one, in fine arts, sponsored by Mead Corporation, the other by Sloan Paper Company to promote better work in advertising art.

Mead's prestigious $25,000 purchase prize "Painting of the Year" was instigated in 1945 by Arthur Harris, then vice president of Mead Corporation. It now tours 16 American cities.

The Greater Atlanta Arts Council unites 85 organizations of the arts joined to develop programs stimulating greater understanding of the arts.

The Council's first Arts Congress in 1967 brought critics and speakers from all over the nation and attracted an attendance of more than 1,700 persons. The Congress has become an annual September event.

The Georgia Art Commission, headed by Atlanta artist George Beattie, was established several years ago to promote the development of the arts in Georgia. It is funded by the state, to match grants from the National Foundation on the Arts and the Humanities to implement art programs throughout the state.

GALLERIES

There has been an explosion of independent galleries for browsing, dreaming and buying. Small and large ones are found throughout the city and its environs. In alphabetical order, they are:

Agnes Scott College
Dana Fine Arts Bldg.,
Decatur
Tel. 373-2571

Allison Art Acres Gallery and School of Art
3940 N. Peachtree Rd.,
Chamblee
Tel. 457-3080

Artists Associates, Inc.
1105 Peachtree St. N.E.
Tel. 892-7681

Atlanta Jewish Community
Center
1745 Peachtree St. N.E.
Tel. 875-7881

Atlanta University Center
Gallery
233 Chestnut St. S.W.
Tel. 523-6431

Briarcliff's La Petite
1230 West Paces Ferry Rd.
N.W.
Tel. 261-5883

Briggs Gallery
798 Peachtree St. N.E.
Tel.874-6219

Brown's Studio Gallery
3120 Roswell Rd. N.W.
Tel. 233-1800

Chelko's New Image Gallery
1166 Peachtree St. N.E.
Tel.892-3427

Dzirkalis Art Gallery
333 Peachtree St. N.E.
Tel. 525-9994

Fine Arts Gallery
1139 Spring St. N.W.
Tel. 876-5610

Galérie Illiene
18 Peachtree Place N.E.
Tel. 874-7268

Gavant Gallery
3889 Peachtree Rd.,
Cherokee Plaza
Tel. 233-3938

Georgia Institute of Technology
School of Architecture,
225 North Ave. N.E.
Tel. 873-4211

Georgia State College Gallery
33 Gilmer St. S.E.
Tel. 577-2400

Heart of Atlanta Motel Gallery
255 Courtland St. N.E.
Tel. 688-1682

Heath's Gallery
62 Ponce de Leon Ave. N.E.
Tel. 876-1468

Herren's Gallery
84 Luckie St. N.W.
Tel. 524-4709

Jens Risom
351 Peachtree Hills Ave.
N.E.
Tel. 237-9223

Little Gallery, Franklin Simon
4th Floor, 640 Peachtree St.
N.E.
Tel. 872-8801

National Bank of Georgia
1430 W. Peachtree St. N.W.
Tel. 523-1461

Picture House, Inc.
1109 W. Peachtree St. N.E.
Tel. 875-9341

Poorman's Gallery
1104 Peachtree St. N.E.
Tel. 892-1271

Rich's
Third Floor, Store for
Homes, Downtown
Tel. 522-4636

S & W Gallery
  1544 Piedmont Rd. N.E.
  Tel. 874-1708

Signature Shop
  3267 Roswell Rd. N.W.
  Tel. 237-4232

Southwest Artists League Gallery
  Fulton Federal Savings and
  Loan Association
  2357 Sewell Rd. S.W.
  Tel. 522-2300

Spelman College Gallery
  Fine Arts Bldg.,
  350 Leonard St. S.W.
  Tel. 523-1056

Stagecoach Gallery
  Stagecoach Manor,
  Ellenwood
  Tel. 366-8984

Unitarian Universalist Congregation
  1911 Cliff Valley Way N.E.
  Tel. 634-5134

Wilens Galleries
  349 Peachtree Hills Ave.
  N.E.
  Tel. 237-2991

MUSEUMS AND COLLECTIONS

Atlanta Historical Society   3099 Andrews Dr. N.W.
  Early Atlanta in pictures, papers, manuscripts, mementoes.
  Franklin Garrett, Director
  Hours: 11 A.M.–3:30 P.M. daily except Saturday; Sundays,
  2–4 P.M.

Atlanta Museum   537 Peachtree St. N.E.
  Furniture, paintings, portraits, silver, some European historical pieces. J. H. Elliott, owner.
  Hours: 10 A.M.–5 P.M. weekdays

Emory Museum   Bishops Hall, Emory Campus
  Middle Eastern objects, Egyptian collection of mummies, coffins, burial jars from the Breasted expedition in 1920; artifacts from Palestine and Israel from archaeological digs of Emory's Dr. Immanuel BenDor.
  Dr. W. B. Baker, Director
  Hours: 10 A.M.–12 noon, Monday–Saturday; 2–4 P.M., Monday–Friday

Executive Center (Governor's Mansion)   391 West Paces
Ferry Rd. N.W.
  Federal-American furnishings of mansion.
  Hours: Monday–Friday, 10 A.M.–1 P.M.; Sundays, 2–5 P.M.

Emory University Library, Special Collections
  One of the finest Confederate Imprints collections in the

country by Keith Reid; the extensive papers of the Joel Chandler Harris family.
David Estes, Librarian
Hours: By appointment

Fulton Federal Savings and Loan Association   21 Edgewood Ave. N.E.
Forty precious and semiprecious gems found in Georgia.
Gilbert W. Withers, Curator and Lecturer
Hours: 9 A.M.–5 P.M., weekdays

Georgia State Museum   State Capitol
Display of natural resources of Georgia, minerals, fossils, Indian relics, small animals
Grey B. Culberson, Director
Hours: 8:30 A.M–4:30 P.M., Monday through Friday; 9:30 A.M.–3:30 P.M., Saturday

High Museum of Art   1280 Peachtree St. N.E.
Collections of old and new art.

Libraries

The Atlanta Public Library, with its 18 branches throughout the city and Fulton County, has more than 700,000 volumes catalogued, as well as a great number of prints, films and records. It has active reference, business and science departments. Carlton Rochelle is Chief Librarian.

One could make a life's work reading the published books of Atlantans and Georgians. These include Conrad Aiken, Erskine Caldwell, Edison Marshall, Lillian Smith, Carson McCullers, Bell Irvin Wiley, Ralph McGill, Berry Fleming, Frank Yerby, Mac Hyman, Ellis Merton Coulter, Elizabeth Stevenson, Flannery O'Connor, Paul Darcy Boles, Tom Ham, Vinnie Williams, Maggie Davis, Celestine Sibley, Harold Martin, Louis E. Lomax, Nancy McLarty, Marion Montgomery, Marguerite Steedman, Thomas J. J. Altizer, Henry T. Malone, William Bailey Williford, Bernice McCullar, Betsy Hopkins Lochridge, Margaret Long, Genevieve Holden, LeGrand Henderson, Douglas Kiker, Pat Watters, Reese Cleghorn, Medora Field Perkerson, Evelyn Hanna, Inez Henry, Elizabeth Anne Ford, Richard Harwell.

Among the poets are James Dickey, formerly consultant in poetry to the Library of Congress, Larry Rubin, John Ransom Lewis, Agnes Cochran Bramlett (Georgia's Poet Laureate), Daniel Whitehead Hickey, Anderson Scruggs, Byron Herbert Reece and Sidney Lanier, minstrel of another time.

The inspirational books of preachers Charles L. Allen and Dow Kirkpatrick, former Atlantans, Robert Ozment, Cecil Myers, Roy O. McClain, Pierce Harris and others are best sellers.

All the schools and colleges have extensive libraries.

Among other valuable acquisitions open to public viewing, Emory University's special collections include a fascinating review of the life and times of the Joel Chandler Harris family and a new collection of the papers of Ralph McGill.

If you happen to revel in history or genealogy, remember the museum and library of the State Capitol and the extensive archives catalogued in the new State Archives Building.

Atlanta is a mecca for archivists. The Federal Records Center in East Point keeps records for seven southeastern states—everything from weather reports to income-tax returns.

On display in this center are the original patents for Eli Whitney's cotton gin, as well as its replica, the draft cards of such famous Americans as Jack Benny, Sinclair Lewis, Cecil B. DeMille, and a significant one belonging to Alvin York, who once protested "I don't want to fight" and went on to become a World War I hero.

British Vice Admiralty records, dating back to 1716, are on display here too, including fascinating accounts of pirate trials.

I I

"The Big One," aluminum
sculpture by Swiss artist Willi
Gutmann, thrusts its two tons
skyward in the Plaza beside
Gas Light Tower.

Five counties make up present-day Metropolitan Atlanta: Fulton, DeKalb, Cobb, Clayton and Gwinnett. Solid lines are county demarcations. Heavy dotted lines show expressway and interstate systems.

History of Atlanta

O F C O U R S E cities have presences. Paris is a silk rose, held in the hands of a great beauty. London is the council chamber of a monarch. Rome is the echoing fanfare of Caesar's legions.

Atlanta is a young man on the go.

The city is paced by a bustle of restless young whirlwinds whose audacity knows no bounds. Many of them are millionaires at thirty.

Forget the myth of matriarchy. That applied to the rural south, where women helped pick up the pieces on plantations after the War Between the States. It never pertained to Atlanta.

Atlanta was frontier men—English, Scots, Welsh, Irish, Jews, all dedicated to the four-letter word WORK.

The place began with a whoop and a holler with rough bearded workingmen, and women who matched their mettle, all of them ready for whatever came.

The first mention of the region is found in Revolutionary War records dated August 1, 1782. It was an account of friction between the Cherokee and Creek Indians at The Standing Peachtree, gateway to northern Cherokee lands.

In 1813 Lieutenant George R. Gilmer (later Governor

of Georgia) and 22 recruits began the first white settlement at The Standing Peachtree.

An engineer's stake marked the place as Terminus. Terminus became Marthasville in 1843. Marthasville became Atlanta two years later—the female version of the word Atlantic.

Two hundred years had already passed in Georgia history.

The Creeks and the Cherokees had first possessed it all. Hernando de Soto, Tristán de Luna, Jean Ribaut and Pedro Menéndez de Avilés had explored it. The Salzburgers, the Moravians, the Scottish Highlanders and the Acadians had come. The Franciscans had brought the faith, the Methodist Wesley brothers, John and Charles, had come and gone, leaving another variety of salvation. Oglethorpe had come and gone, and King George had been proclaimed King in Savannah.

A newspaper had been issued, a constitution ratified, the British had been expelled, the University of Georgia chartered and a second constitution had been adopted. The Yazoo scandal had occurred, gold had been discovered, the George railroad chartered, Emory, Mercer and the Georgia Female Colleges had been founded.

The Creeks and the Cherokees had been relieved of their land and removed from the state. The first operation under anesthesia had been performed and the State Sanitarium for the Insane had been established.

Clearly, this city was a late bloomer, but it was born running.

All Atlanta was, really, was energy applied to geography. It was the shortest distance between supply and demand, between commerce and customers. It was simply a mathematical fact.

In his admirable volumes *Atlanta and Environs,* historian and City biographer Franklin Garrett explained: "The railroads wanted traffic and the town wanted trade and travel. They combined their energies and enterprising spirits to boost each other. New citizens began to accumulate and enter into business engagements. Denizens of the region began to make Atlanta their marketplace."

From the beginning, Atlanta gave itself no airs. The slave-plantation society around it was flowering, but Atlanta's social life was built to suit the brawling satisfactions of hog drovers, mule traders and steel drivers.

The years that led up to the Civil War and the burning of Atlanta were busy. The town was made county seat of a newly carved area named Fulton. The Athenaeum Theater was opened, the first city hall built. The Holland Free School opened, and the Atlanta Medical College was founded.

The tension between the North and South began to build in Atlanta, and by the late 1850s, industrialists considered sending their products to Europe for sale, rather than attempting commerce with their Yankee critics.

When Georgia seceded from the Union on January 19, 1861, Atlanta was placed under Confederate martial law. It became the supply depot for the Confederacy, a manufacturing, military and hospitalization center. As many as 80,000 wounded soldiers were brought to Atlanta to be treated and quartered.

On July 22, 1863, the Battle of Atlanta began in the southeastern part of the city. Guns were hauled down from Chattanooga; a siege followed. Atlanta was bombarded for two months, with all communications lost except the Central Railroad.

When General Sherman defeated General W. J. Hardee in the Battle of Jonesboro and seized the railroad, Atlanta's fate was sealed.

The same providential resource that had established it in the first place—geography—had marked it for destruction.

The Yankees burned Atlanta.

When General Sherman and his army resumed their march toward the sea, they had dispersed all of Atlanta's surviving population to the south and razed all but some 400 of the town's 4,500 houses and commercial buildings.

The soul-shriveling agonies of a city's immolation are a

Georgia General Assembly in session during regime of Governor Carl Sanders as he spoke to State Senate.

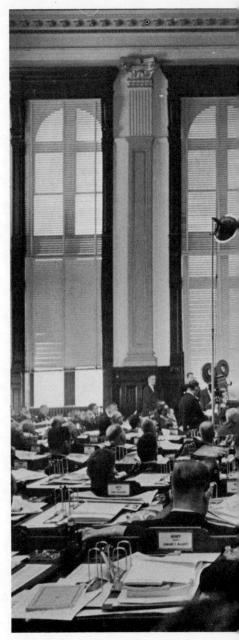

kind of crucifixion. The records of the exodus and survival are purest anguish. It was a time of unspeakable horror, of orgies and excesses and looting and drunkenness, of hate and cruelty and savagery. People lived in tunnels they dug in banks of railroad cuts, or in gopher holes in small hollows in back yards. Prices climbed to unbelievable figures. Bacon was $500 a pound; salt, $100 a pound. A mixture of cereals and sawdust pretended to be coffee.

The late Margaret Mitchell was the first Atlantan to help the city put this war into perspective and to see itself as it must have always been—envied, strong and indomitable.

A hundred years later, people all over the world wept when they read *Gone With The Wind,* and wrote loving commiserations to Atlanta officials.

The Reconstruction was a scourging time, but amidst it many opportunities were seized and fortunes were begun.

Liberated Negroes were given their first education under the Freedman's Bureau. The first Board of Education was elected in 1870; three years later, public schools were opened to 4,000 children.

The first mule-drawn streetcars began to operate in 1874, creating the first of Atlanta's famous traffic jams.

Atlanta became the capital city of Georgia in 1868, after offering the state free office space for ten years as well as a capitol site.

As the capital of the state, Atlanta has been the focus of politics, majestic or absurd, as the case may be. It has provided three mansions (a fourth one was leased for a time) which have housed heads of state of varying distinction.

One governor, Rufus Bulloch, absconded when he faced impeachment in 1871. They counted the silverware in the mansion. He returned later and became a sterling citizen once more.

Another, Alexander Hamilton Stephens, "Little Alec," Vice President of the Confederacy, became governor in 1882 while an invalid. He died five months later, having worked at his duties as governor only about a week.

One governor, John M. Slaton, became a martyr when he commuted the death sentence of Leo Frank, convicted in the murder of Mary Fagan. This ruined Slaton's political future, but assured him a place in Georgia history.

Once this state, in a peak of plenitude, had TWO governors at one time.

For the past century the city has been the scene of the General Assembly each winter for six exciting weeks. While it has often viewed with a mixture of contempt and disbelief the goings-on at the statehouse, where its destinies have been decided along with the cities and towns of 158 other counties in this state of more than 4,000,000 citizens, the people of Atlanta have ever been fascinated by the elocution, folklore and effusive salutations expressed in the real-life dramas at the capitol.

Crowded visitors' galleries always respond with applause to the legislative customs inherited from olde England of Magna Carta days.

For example, no matter how jugular have been the maneuverings of the day, the Speaker of the House always leaves the rostrum on the run, pausing to bow with mock dignity to his colleagues as he dashes from the chamber to the sound of cheering.

Politics is neither dull nor predictable in the Capital of Georgia.

Atlanta Today

ATLANTA IS governed now in a unicameral system headed by a Mayor and a Board of Aldermen, composed of two aldermen from each of the city's eight wards.

Aldermen are responsible for the operation of the city's 20 departments, with the exception of the Departments of Personnel and Public Library. These operate under their own citizens boards.

The public schools, operated under the direction of an elected Board of Education are a separate part of the city government. All funds of the school department are handled by the Board of Education, composed of nine members —one from each of the eight wards and one from the city at large. They serve four-year terms.

The city operates its own sewage disposal system, airport and waterworks.

The Chattahoochee River, aided by the establishment of dams and the impoundment of southern-bound waters at Lake Lanier, supplies Atlanta with what is claimed to be the softest water in the United States. The city's water plans will be adequate for two million citizens as things now stand.

Atlanta's political system is of the type known in urban governing circles as the Weak Mayor system, but the city has, in fact, thrived under strong, uncommon men as mayors.

One of the most recent of these has been William B. Hartsfield, a patriarch with a pixie wit who retired in 1961 after 24 years. He was succeeded by Ivan Allen, Jr., successful business executive, whose commercial vision and social insight have impressed his constituents.

This community has the oldest publicly supported regional planning group in the United States. The Atlanta Region Metropolitan Planning Commission has been functioning here since 1947, working toward solutions of problems that do not stop at county lines or city limits.

The city itself has a Planning Department. In 1968 it adopted a Master Land Use Plan for 1983, when the city is expected to be the hub of a metropolis of 2,000,000 persons.

This metropolis is now fragmented into 45 municipalities, five counties, nine school districts, 23 sewer systems, 38 water systems and several authorities.

Increasing discussion of the need for a metropolitan government of some kind was still, in 1969, in the hinting stage.

Streets and roads have always been a problem in Atlanta since the 1840s, when, in rainy seasons, wagons sank to their hubs in the mud, and mules balked in their tracks.

The most pressing concern in the area is still the movement of people and vehicles. Atlanta's extensive system of expressways and a circumferential road encompassing the city grow ever more crowded as the population surges.

The Metropolitan Atlanta Rapid Transit Authority—MARTA—has plans for a basic rapid transit system and construction of a coordinated system using busways and railways.

Social planning for Atlanta is performed largely by the Community Council, an agency of the United Appeal.

The city operates about 11,000 units of public housing, with new units constantly under construction as part of the city's urban-renewal program.

Atlanta led the nation in 1933 with the first housing projects for low income citizens. Under the leadership of realtor Charles Palmer and "under thunderheads of adversity" more than ten blocks of slums were razed and replaced with 600 apartments in that depression year.

Atlanta has achieved one of the most ambitious urban-renewal records in America in the last eleven years under the Atlanta Housing Authority.

The program had, in early 1969, involved more than $240 million in Federal and local funds, with 13 separate projects in work involving almost 6,000 acres of land.

The city's new blitz-built stadium and its new Civic Center stand on redeveloped property. Georgia State College, Georgia Tech, Atlanta University and Howard High School are among the educational institutions that have expanded with urban renewal.

The city's police force is headed by Herbert Turner Jenkins, who considers his force of 900 uniformed men, 150 or so civilians and 125 school traffic patrolwomen the best disciplined police corps in the world.

Chief P. O. Williams leads the city fire department's corps of almost 900 firemen with 34 single and 15 double companies operating from 33 fire stations. The Atlanta Fire Department also serves portions of Fulton County under special contract.

The city has an exceptional financial record. City bonds bring a premium, and in the last 30 years, Atlanta has not borrowed a dollar for operating expenses.

Atlanta is the seat of Fulton County, which is governed by three Commissioners of Roads and Revenue, with a County Manager, whom they appoint.

The county operates family and children's services and health services for the entire area, including Atlanta. It operates its own separate school system under a board of education appointed by the grand jury. Paul D. West is Superintendent of County Schools.

Atlanta is the Federal Government's southeastern regional capital with thousands of government employees in many branches of Federal service. Among the many large Federal installations here are the Army's General Depot at Conley, Dobbins Air Force Base at Marietta, the headquarters of the Third Army at Fort McPherson and the Public Health Services' Communicable Disease Center. This is also the regional headquarters for the Internal Revenue Service and for the Social Security agency.

There are three major career consuls in Atlanta, supplemented by fourteen honorary counsuls serving as liaison between foreign governments and the United States and assisting nationals of other lands with their problems of business, citizenship, passports and other foreign-service functions. The honorary consulate group is comprised, in most cases, of natives of the countries they represent, though they are now citizens of the United States. If they are not natives of the foreign lands, they have an interest in the nation they represent for one reason or another.

CAREER CONSULS:

Germany:	Roland Gottlieb, Consul 1210 Fulton National Bank Bldg.	Tel. 525-2097
Israel:	Zeev Boneh, Consul General 805 Peachtree Bldg.	Tel. 875-7851
United Kingdom:	S. H. Anstey, Consul General 8th Floor, Merchandise Mart Bldg.	Tel. 524-2691

HONORARY CONSULS:

Austria:	Robert Bunzl, Consul General 609 Red Rock Bldg.	Tel. 688-2505
Belgium:	Henry L. deGive, Consul Healey Bldg.	Tel. 524-4704

Bolivia:	Gustavo Estenssoro, Consul	Tel. 938-5343
	2145 Serpentine Dr. N.E.	
Costa Rica:	Mrs. Rose Cunningham, Consul	Tel. 634-7759
	1232 Arborvista Dr. N.E.	
Denmark:	John C. Portman, Jr.	Tel. 522-8811
	2107 Peachtree Center Bldg.	
El Salvador:	Joe Howell, Consul	Tel. 873-2163
	1776 Peachtree Bldg., Suite 614	
France:	Arthur Harris, Consular Agent	Tel. 876-6264
	950 W. Marietta St. N.W.	
Guatemala:	Mrs. Maria A. Fraser, Consul	Tel. 255-7019
	4772 E. Conway Dr. N.W.	
Italy:	John Fornara, Vice Consul	Tel. 875-6177
	1106 W. Peachtree St. N.E.	
Mexico:	Robert E. Shivers, Jr.	Tel. 355-4901
	1185 Collier Rd. N.W.	
Monaco:	Carling Dinkler, Jr.,	Tel. 524-2461
	98 Forsyth Street N.W.	
Panama:	Jorge Tzafaras, Vice Consul	Tel. 457-0589
	P. O. Box 7304	
Sweden:	Burke Dowling Adams, Consul	Tel. 875-0121
	1750 Peachtree Rd. N.W.	
Uruguay:	Mrs. Jack Adair, Consul	Tel. 237-0651
	290 Argonne Dr. N.W.	

TRADE OFFICES:

Government of Ontario:	Harry R. Nellis	Tel. 577-1883
	230 Peachtree St. N.W.	

Transportation, Industry and Business

Call it pragmatism, enlightened self-interest, smart business or plain old avarice, the thing that makes Atlanta tick is the pot of gold.

We see the rainbow and we love its melting colors. But the part we like best is that prize at the end.

If Atlanta were to be named a fourth time it would simply have a few letters added and become Atlanta, Incorporated.

The city is a humming capital company with 1,300,000 stockholders, more or less, all conditioned by birth, environment and disposition to the same basic stimuli: the happy jingle of the cash register.

Since the day it began, Atlanta has thrived on the deal, the trade, the service, the product, the satisfaction, all of these turned toward the fulfillment of its people.

Take the Forward Atlanta syndrome.

The first manifestation came in 1880. It was a slow year, so the city fathers proposed an International Cotton Exposition to promote the image of the city.

It was a success. They tried it again. And again. And again. And again. They were all successes.

The sixth Forward Atlanta campaign was undertaken in 1965. This commitment is now in its second three-year phase. The objective remains the same: to accelerate by national advertising the importance of Atlanta as *the* major manufacturing and distribution center of the Southeast.

The secret of Atlanta's success is its location. Its people have always known it. That's why they came here in the first place. They have stayed for other reasons.

Transportation

The first iron horse Atlanta ever saw was a trumped-up affair that chugged from Marthasville to Marietta on Christmas Eve, 1842. It traveled on rails that "didn't start nowhere or go nowhere" and it was the marvel of the century. Everybody on board celebrated with syllabub made strong with Madeira wine.

Railroads created excitement, fortunes and a sense of destiny in Atlanta.

Early railroad men slept on bearskins in shanties. Their successors slept in mansions as millionaires.

Now six major roads operate into and out of Atlanta over 13 lines. Eighty-eight railroads maintain offices here. For 100 years Atlanta has been the railroad center of the Southeast.

Fifty-two passenger trains a day depart from two terminals, and more than 350,000 freight cars are loaded annually. In addition to these, approximately 300 merchandise and package cars originate daily in Atlanta.

Ribbon track, television scanning, radar speed sensing, analogous computers and elaborate communications are in use by Atlanta railroads, which have spent $200 million or more in refurbishments in the South over the past ten years.

The missing spoke in Atlanta's transportation wheel is the waterway. The old Chattahoochee is big enough but it has many a lurch and plunge between Atlanta and the Gulf of Mexico.

However, there are already 260 miles of open channel from the Gulf to Columbus, Georgia, about a hundred miles to the southwest of Atlanta, and studies, discussions, plans for more waterways go on all the time.

The impossible takes a little longer.

Aircraft

The Air Age came earlier to Atlanta than it did to the rest of the nation.

It was up, up and away in their beautiful balloon for

World's biggest plane, the C5 Galaxy built at Lockheed-Georgia in Marietta, cruises by Stone Mountain, largest example of exposed granite in the world, five miles in circumference.

Executive Park, an office park that is unique in the nation, seen from the air over I-85

Dr. Albert Hape and Professor Samuel A. King, two gentlemen of the highest sporting blood, on December 10, 1869.

Six thousand people stood on housetops and jammed Marietta Street to see the test of the "Hyperion."

The "Hyperion" zigged, zagged, soared upward a mile, and could still be seen speeding on its buoyant journey. The two balloonists dined, drank and played a bugle aloft. The music drifted through the clouds. A church meeting, hearing the strains, decided that the world was coming to an end and they were hearing Gabriel himself blowing his horn.

Even discounting the Great Balloon Launching, Atlanta led the air age. In 1911, Lindsey Hopkins of Atlanta bought the first biplane sold by the Curtiss Company. Mr. Hopkins and a companion flew from Nassau, New York, to Mineola Field in the Atlantan's new plane, and Hopkins mailed Atlanta's first airmail letter to the *Atlanta Constitution*. It was dated October 2, 1911.

The Atlanta Airport, completed in 1961 at a cost of $60

million, is now underway in a $200 to $300 million expansion program. More than 750 scheduled passenger and cargo flights arrive and depart the airport daily, serving 74 cities nonstop, making Atlanta the fourth busiest airport in the nation in passenger enplanements and fifth in departures.

The city is served by seven airlines: Delta, Eastern, Northwest, Piedmont, Southern, Trans-World and United. Delta and Southern base their operations here. Eastern operates its largest connecting terminal here. Twenty-one airlines have Atlanta offices. It is the region's (and one of the nation's) largest air freight terminals.

There are 11 secondary airports in the five-county area, six private, three public and two military installations, which accommodate all types of aircraft from crop-dusters to multi-engine transports. They include the Fulton County Airport; Cobb Airpark, Marietta; DeKalb-Peachtree Airport, Chamblee; Dobbins Air Force Base, Marietta; Ted Edwards Skyport, Palmetto; Gunn Airfield, Lithonia; McCullum Airport, Marietta; Morris Army Airfield, Atlanta General Depot, Forest Park; Parkaire, Marietta; Stone Mountain Airport, Stone Mountain; and South Expressway Airport, Jonesboro.

Automobiles

The horseless carriage also came early to Atlanta.

In 1901, three locomobile steamers weighing 640 pounds apiece made their maiden journey in Atlanta—nine miles in two hours.

Now Ford's Georgia plants have turned out more than two million vehicles. Atlanta also has a Chevrolet Fisher body plant, a Chevrolet parts depot and a huge General Motors Plant, assembling Buicks, Oldsmobiles and Chevrolets.

Buses

The first stagecoach stop was Whitehall Inn in West End in the early 1840's, with stages driven by four-horse teams, and the driver himself acting as a kind of human grapevine. Watching him hitch up a new span of horses drew children for miles.

Now seven bus lines serve Atlanta from two downtown terminals, with more than 430 big fellows entering and leaving the city daily, carrying 81,000 or more passengers.

Trailways has a posh new six-story multimillion-dollar terminal on Spring Street from which its buses, as well as those of Smoky Mountain Trailways, Continental Trailways, Tamiami Trailways and the Tennessee Coach Trailways operate.

The Greyhound Lines has regional offices here and is now building a new terminal adjacent to the Civic Center. Its terminal is also used by Southeastern Stages, Inc., and Southeastern Motor Lines.

Trucks

More than 170 regulated motor carriers now serve points in 36 states from Atlanta, with direct service available to most of them east of the Mississippi River. They operate 75 terminals and do not include the hundreds of trucks bringing perishables to the Atlanta Farmers Market, and thousands of private truck operators who haul their own products.

In addition to transportation and distribution, Atlanta's balanced mix includes manufacturing, merchandising, finance, government and business services.

Of the 500 largest industrial corporations in America, 100 make or assemble a product in Atlanta, 220 maintain warehouses, and 400 have sales or service offices, most of them regional in scope. More than 3,500 commodities are produced here by some 1,650 manufacturers.

A few of the industrial giants who call Atlanta home are Coca-Cola, Delta Air Lines, the Retail Credit Company, the Southern Company, Scripto, Colonial Stores, Rollins Corp., Fuqua Industries, Genuine Parts, Butler Shoes, National Service Industries, Inc., and The Rushton Company.

The largest single employer and biggest industrial giant in the Southeast is Lockheed-Georgia in metro Atlanta's Marietta, where the world's largest plane, the C-5 Galaxy, is made, as well as the Hercules and Lockheed Starlifters. The plant has a $200 million annual payroll.

Lockheed has deep and wide involvements in the industrial fabric of the South and ranges throughout the world for manufacturing services. The wings of its recently introduced Galaxy were subcontracted in England with 1,000 British aerospace engineers in constant IBM hot-line communication with the Lockheed-Georgia engineering force in Marietta.

BANKING

Atlanta is banker for the South and fiscal agent for the United States.

A long and boisterous battle was waged in 1913 with 200 other cities in the United States for a banking prize—the establishment of the first Federal Reserve Bank in the South. Atlanta won the boardroom standdown for this banker's bank and is still counting the blessings and profits from emerging victor in the power struggle in the Sixth Federal Reserve District.

Its first largest banks, the First National, Citizens and Southern, Fulton National, National Bank of Georgia and the Trust Company of Georgia, all have their own skyscraper buildings and numerous branches. Metro Atlanta has 44 banks with resources upward of $3 billion.

The history of the savings and loan association is a long and successful one. Twenty-one such associations operate in the five-county area, with assets totaling more than a billion dollars.

Forty firms engage in investment underwriting, brokerage activities and investment counseling in Atlanta. One of the largest of these is Courts and Company, Atlanta based, founded in 1925.

Real estate has always been a kingmaker in Atlanta. Construction and development have made recent dramatic fortunes.

The hang-up of the last decade has been the structural crane. The horizon is spiked with them, raising their claws into the air as if a family of mechanical insects were practicing an outsize ballet.

The city's frenetic building pace has inspired the Wit's End players to perform a rollocking skit and song entitled "They're Tearing Up Peachtree Again."

Nobody laughs as hard as the folks who live in the area.

From the commercial real-estate point of view, Executive Park is a dramatic case in point.

Executive Park is an office park, unique in the nation, developed by J. Michael Gearon, a young Atlantan. Until 1964, when it was bought for about $13,000 an acre, dairy cows had grazed on its 122-acre meadow. Now this land sells for as much as $225,000 an acre, has many national tenants, and operates its own hotels and other services.

Industrial parks are further proof. There are many of these.

Great Southwest Industrial Park, the second largest industrial park in the nation, covers 3,000 acres. It will be the address of 1,500 different companies housed in half a billion dollars' worth of buildings. It has its own contemporary sculpture gardens. Construction workmen recently uncovered archaeological findings of such importance in its area that a part of Great Southwest has now been set aside as a historical site while the digging continues into what now appear to be pre-Columbian remains.

Fulton Industrial Park, operated by the Fulton County government, adjoins Great Southwest. It covers 2,000 acres, was opened in 1948 and is now developed almost to capacity with more than 90 plants.

Peachtree City is 16,000 acres of beautiful property, 30 miles from downtown Atlanta in Fayette County. It is completely preplanned and zoned for a complete city. The Bessemer Properties, Inc., envision its completion by the year 2000.

RETAILING

Retailing is a major business. Atlanta ranks 21st in total retail sales and 24th in consumer spendable income in the nation. Over a third of Georgia's buying income is in Atlanta, more than three billion dollars.

One store alone, Rich's, which some of us think is the "most" store east of the sun and west of the moon, does an annual business in excess of $170 million in its six outlets here. It is the South's largest department store.

Davison's, a Macy affiliate, with three of its Georgia stores in Atlanta; Sears, Roebuck and Company's Southern headquarters offices, and five department stores and 30 special service outlets; J. C. Penney, with traditional and full-line stores as well as Treasure Island outlets; specialty stores such as J. P. Allen's, Regenstein's, Muse's, Parks-Chambers, all native Atlanta merchants, and those from elsewhere; Saks Fifth Avenue, Brooks Brothers, Franklin Simon, Peck and Peck; discount stores such as K-Mart, Arlans, Zayres, GEX, Treasure Island, Atlantic, Gibson, Grant City, Woolco, serve Atlanta now and plan to double their retailing space by 1983 to a 100 million square feet to serve the city's estimated two million population.

More than 100 shopping centers are here, six of them regional in scope. Despite these, downtown Atlanta is still the largest and most complete shopping center. About a fifth of the total retail sales are made downtown.

A horde of manpower services, including one for workers over 40 years of age, help fill the 100,000 new jobs created over the last five years.

Cylindrical bronze Citizens and Southern National Bank, North Avenue branch, situated opposite Life of Georgia. Nestling at right is All Saints Episcopal Church with the Varsity Drive-In and Grant Field behind it. Coca Cola's new building stands in distance.

INSURANCE

More than 850 insurance companies operate in Georgia, including 80 state-based companies. Almost all have offices in Atlanta, and not the least of these is the Life of Georgia's multimillion-dollar skyscraper on North Avenue, the Equitable Life Assurance Society's new 34-story building, and its nearby neighbor, the Hartford Life Insurance Building.

WHOLESALING

Atlanta is the storage and distribution point of the Southeast.

Six years ago the $15 million, 23-story Atlanta Merchandise Mart opened with a million square feet of floor space under one roof. This space has now been doubled to accommodate the wholesale needs of the Mart's tenants, who display chiefly floor coverings, furniture, gifts, apparel and household accessories.

Atlanta holds 11th position as a wholesaling center and is especially strong in such commodities as drugs, chemicals, drygoods, electrical goods, motor vehicles and automotive equipment, and furniture.

WAREHOUSING

Warehousing is big business. More than 30 public warehousing firms supply clients throughout the Southeast. Refrigerated warehouse facilities constantly expand to meet the demand of frozen food storage. The city has the largest completely refrigerated motor truck line in the world.

Atlanta is not the somnolent South. It is not sorghum syrup, fatback and hoecake. It is camellias, corporations and cash.

Outsiders simply don't believe it. Every one of them has to discover it for himself. Having done so, their enthusiasm is the reflection of their own great discovery:

Atlanta is a new kind of city!

White columns on West Peachtree, picturesque home of WSB-Television and WSB-Radio

Press, Radio, Television, Advertising

Atlanta gets the message. It is the communication nerve center of the Southeast.

The *Atlanta Constitution* has been publishing since June 16, 1868, when President Andrew Johnson gave the paper its name and gave Carey Wentworth Styles permission to publish to "help restore dignity and constitutional government to a prostrate people."

The *Atlanta Journal* has been here almost as long. The *Journal* will be a century old in 1983.

Jointly owned and published since 1950, The Atlanta Newspapers, Inc., have won five Pulitzer prizes. On Sundays they serve well over half a million readers.

President of the two newspapers is Jack Tarver. Reg Murphy is editor of the *Atlanta Constitution*, of which the late Ralph McGill was the celebrated long-time editor and publisher. Jack Spalding is editor of the *Atlanta Journal*. Central interest in the newspapers remains in the family of James M. Cox.

The oldest paper in the metro area, the *Marietta Journal*, has recorded the life and times of Cobb County for 103 years.

The *Atlanta Daily World*, the only daily newspaper published and owned by Negroes in the United States, also publishes newspapers for eight Southern cities from its office on Auburn Street. Under the editorship of W. S. Scott, his younger brother, C. A. Scott, his sons and other members of the Scott Family, the *Daily World* has won many journalistic honors, including the Capital Press Award as newspaper of the year for valiant service in the cause of civil rights.

Twenty-two weekly newspapers are published in the community, two of them with special ethnic appeal. The *Southern Israelite* concentrates on news of specific Jewish interest. The *Atlanta Inquirer* deals mainly with community news for Negro readers.

Two worldwide news-gathering agencies have Southeastern bureaus here. The Atlanta Bureau for the Associated Press is the control point for news emanating from Alabama, Florida, Georgia, Louisiana, Mississippi and Tennessee. News and pictures are sent to, and received from, the rest of the world. United Press International's Southern Division headquarters, central office for eight states, edits and relays news to UPI subscribers and bureaus in the Southeast.

The Georgia Press Association, representing daily, weekly and biweekly newspapers, has its headquarters here. The GPS's October Cracker Crumble, a musical production lampooning politics for the benefit of journalism scholarships, is worth splurging on.

The following have regional offices in Atlanta: *The New York Times, Washington Post, Los Angeles Times, Wall Street Journal, Fairchild Publications, Newsweek, Business Week, Time.*

Several major Georgia newspapers maintain bureaus here including the *Savannah Morning News and Press*, the *Athens Banner Herald*, the *Augusta Chronicle and Herald*, the *Columbus Ledger and Inquirer*, the *Macon Telegraph and News*.

Most of the major broadcasting networks and newspaper publishers are represented in Atlanta.

Approximately 40 trade journals and industrial magazines are printed here. The oldest publisher in the field is McFadden Business Publications, established in 1903. Two industrial journals devoted to advertising are *Southern Markets* and *Media and Southern Advertising*.

The Georgia Magazine is published here, with Mrs. Ann Lewis as editor. *The Chattahoochee*, an international non-academic quarterly magazine, is published under the editorship of Eugene Moore.

Three of the universities, Atlanta, Emory and Georgia Tech, publish academic quarterlies, and Georgia State College publishes an economic review.

Among book publishers are W. R. C. Smith Publishing Company, largest publishing house in the Southeast; Tupper and Love, Inc.; Camelot Publishing Company; and the Harrison Company. Harrison is the only publisher of law books south of Virginia.

The Atlanta News Agency, of which Edward E. Elson is President, maintains a network of distribution outlets for all national magazines and periodicals and newspapers, including out-of-town papers and a broad assortment of paperback books.

Atlanta has six television stations: WAGA (CBS), Channel 5; WQXI (ABC) Channel 11; WSB (NBC) Channel 2, two educational stations, the University of Georgia's

WGTV, Channel 8, and the Atlanta Board of Education's WETV, Channel 30 (UHF), and another UHF station, WJRJ, Channel 17.

WSB and WAGA, the two oldest stations, are each housed in stately pillared buildings, WSB's business home being known as "White Columns."

The unique Protestant Radio and Television Center at 1727 Clifton Road, N. E., is the world's largest production and distribution center for non-commercial religious and educational films, audio and video tapes and disc recordings. More than 30 denominations participate in programs distributed to 2200 radio and television stations throughout the network.

In 1922 radio crackled in when the *Atlanta Journal*'s WSB went on the air with 100 watts. "The boys in Hudgins store, 30 miles to the north" heard it clearly.

There are now 30 AM and FM radio stations, including two educational broadcasters. Those with both FM and AM are WAVO, WGKA, WPLO and WSB, the latter now clear-channeling it with 50,000 watts.

WSB won its first George Foster Peabody award for distinguished public service in 1947 and has since acquired four more Peabody prizes.

A 15-mile stretch of Peachtree Street is the region's Madison Avenue, with 40 of the city's 60 advertising agencies having Peachtree addresses. Most of the major New York agencies have Atlanta branches. The two largest Atlanta-based agencies are Tucker Wayne and Company and Liller, Neal, Battle and Lindsey, Inc. Total advertising billings are now pushing the $100 million mark.

Atlanta's graphic arts industry—printing, engraving, stereotyping, trade binding, packaging, paper manufacturing, commercial art and photography—is broad, complete and often prize-winning.

W. R. Bean and Son prints three portions of *Time* magazine here each week. The Foote and Davies Division of McCall Corporation prints 1,750,000 copies of TV Guide for the 13-state Southern region.

Busy, busy, busy Atlanta is a telephone-communication vortex. The Metropolitan dialing area is the largest geographical tollfree dialing service in the world, with Southern Bell's network providing direct connections to all major cities in the United States.

Western Union, which first stuttered in in 1830, following the railroads, ranks fourth in the nation in message volume and revenue. All messages originating in Georgia, Florida and the Carolinas pass through Atlanta's office.

Latest to come have been film and television production studios, establishing a little Culver City off Peachtree. Five audiovisual production and film agencies have complete facilities for photography, tapes, animated film strips, motion pictures of all types; they even turn out custom composition of musical scores and accompaniments.

If it's worth telling anybody, we can help you do it in Atlanta.

Peachtree Street looking north with Peachtree Center in the foreground

III

Everyone's dream well describes this white-columned home with flowering trees and rolling green lawn on scenic tour of Atlanta's northwest residential section.

Rolling terrain and dogwoods, hollies, azaleas and other flowering trees and shrubs indigenous to the region help make lovely home settings such as these.

How and Where We Live

IF YOU are planning to come to live in Atlanta, you have something pleasant in your future.

Atlanta's residential sections are probably the handsomest in America. Gentle undulations, forests of trees, boundless space and money make a wonderful alliance.

One can live in a mansion surrounded by acres of green velvet and cloud-high pine trees, downtown in a skyscraper encircled with interstate highways, commute fifty miles in any direction on the spokes and perimeter of Atlanta's expressway system, go home to a yacht, a private fish pond, or forty-acres-and-a-mule.

If you're a peat moss and pine straw buff, the suburbs may be for you. We have dozens of them. Strangers flatter us by saying they're especially impressive with their manicured greenswards and vistas fit for a Versailles courtesan. But why not? The mowers hardly ever stop running.

If you're the kind who turns on after five, you'd like to dwell in an aerie 20 stories up and look down on the glitter and twinkle that is a modern city when the lights come on.

The nightscapes are incredible. We're building these eagle's nests all over the city.

If you're somewhere between rural and urban, think of townhouses. We have one block of townhouses, the Baltimore Block, that has been here since 1885. But the automobile doomed the Baltimore Block as a tiny Georgetown. No one could find a place to park the Mercedes except in the garden. That left no place for unicorns, water fountains or tree roses.

Now the Baltimore Block is a haven for coffeehouses and arty gatherings, but the idea of townhouses has spread. Townhouses spring up in some untownish places, some of them 30 miles from Five Points.

These privately owned dwellings with a common-wall relationship, are practical and popular. They share heated swimming pools, saunas and sometimes even a golf course, a tennis court or a riding ring. For that you might sacrifice trimming your Zoysia, heady as that joy might be.

Atlanta has a floating suburb with more than 200 houseboats on Lake Lanier. Many people with year-round houses on the rims of Lanier, Allatoona or Lake Berkeley (which is an incorporated town) commute back and forth from downtown morning and night.

You can turn your back on Atlanta and its suburbs and go home to one of the tree-shaded streets of our neighboring towns. Snellville, Norcross, Villa Rica, Duluth, Mableton, Forest Park, Griffin, Newnan and such places have enough compensations to wipe out the memory of the trip to and fro if your daily assignment is in the heart of Atlanta.

Atlanta is growing in all directions. If statistics would stand still, we would tell you how many new houses and apartments have been built since yesterday, but they won't.

Home building has become the city's largest industry. While more than 70 percent of the families live in single-family houses, we're building more apartments all the time. Most of the newer ones are complete communities with recreational facilities of every kind, entertainment rooms and other luxuries unheard of by the most decadent sybarites of the past.

A recent survey showed Atlanta to have the lowest construction cost for houses of similar quality of 13 metropolitan areas.

This book cannot advise you where to live. That is a matter of your requirements, money, taste and responsibilities. We suggest you drive or be driven around considerably before you make up your mind. Look, listen and feel. There is quite a difference in values, depending upon the section you choose.

Atlanta is made up of quarters whose residents have friendly dealings with other communities but reserve their loyalties for their own little neighborhoods. Surrounding the city are dozens of small towns, all a part of the metropolitan entity, possessing their own independence and, most of all, their own attitudes and points of view.

The City Government of Atlanta learns this anew every time it mentions expanding city limits by annexation. A flirtation between settlements is fine, but political marriage is another matter.

In the crescendo of a colorful century, communities have come and gone. Some of these have come back again and others seem on the way.

Boldly, we'll choose two commonly conceded as the most assured: Buckhead and Ansley Park.

Until late 1967, Ansley Park was dominated in a sense by the stone fortress inhabited by Georgia's governors since 1924. The community is five minutes by expressway from the business heart of Atlanta, a spacious medley of mellow old houses surmounting hilltops, snug bungalows tucked in vales and some surprising new residences, all facing a maze of streets winding in and out among parks and groves.

You can get lost in Ansley Park, but you'll enjoy it.

Buckhead is an aura more than a territory. It is an amorphous group of affluent addresses with N.W. or N.E. after them and an indefinable air of having arrived. It is West

Snipes get ready for University Yacht Club Regatta at Lake Lanier, just a pleasant drive from Atlanta.

Paces Ferry, Nancy's Creek, West Wesley, Habersham, Rivers Road, Andrews, Peachtree Battle, Tuxedo, Blackland and dozens of other names that need no explanation to anyone who has been here a while.

This portion of the city began as 202½ acres bought in 1838 for $650. Now a fragment of residential land with a mere 100-foot frontage might cost as much as $36,000. It has been only lately that land could be bought in such small parcels.

If being cherished by those who know it best, its own residents, is any criterion, Brookwood Hills should be in this group, too. People who live there wouldn't trade their Georgian homes and city-sized yards for all the elegance and responsibilities of Buckhead's Valley Road.

Cascade-Campbellton is on the southwest side of Atlanta. It is the fastest-growing section in huge Fulton

County, expanding with pleasant, impressive houses even faster than Sandy Springs to the north.

Sandy Springs, which most people concede is the nearest thing this area has to a Westchester County, has developed from about 5,000 residents living in quiet withdrawal in 1950 to at least 40,000, most of them in the upper brackets of executivedom. Homes range from a modest $25,000 on a tree-shaded lot to estate plots of five or more acres with houses costing $100,000 and up that include lovely views of the Chattahoochee River.

Tenth Street is Atlanta's Little Bohemia, its nearest thing to Greenwich Village. It was once known as "Tight Squeeze," a name it won in the evil days of Reconstruction when that was what it took to get through its dark passageways and convoluted streets with one's life. Later it was known as Blooming Hill. Its two outstanding enterprises in that era were a liquor establishment owned by a man named Rough Rice and, reasonably enough, a Temperance Hall.

Then there are Sherwood Forest, Garden Hills, Morningside, Crestwood, Hunter Road, Peyton Forest-Cascade, West End, dozens of "Manors," "Parks," "Hills," "Heights" and "Circles," all with their own unique cachet.

This, of course, doesn't delineate a city, but it will give you a general idea of the variety of architecture and a sense of time and place.

Outside Atlanta, several towns are haughtily aware of their historic seniority.

Decatur is a city of 25,000, a strong, stable, self-possessed community with the highest education level and the highest per capita income per family in the area. It is the capital of thriving DeKalb County and is far more than Atlanta's bedroom, as any Decaturite will quickly tell you.

Marietta, like Decatur, predates Atlanta and has had an interesting life. It began with one log dwelling in 1832 when Stephen Harrison Long, the railroad engineer who established the location of Atlanta, decided he'd rather live in Marietta. Marietta became the capital of Cobb County and also the neighboring village to other settlements in Cobb known by names now forgotten: Sweet Water Town, Kennesau Town and Buffalo Fish Town. Marietta is known nationally as the address of Lockheed-Georgia's aircraft facility.

Norcross, now the center of a rapidly growing residential community in Gwinnett County, and a prospective terminal point for Atlanta's proposed rapid transit system, was a beautiful village known best as a summer resort a century ago. J. J. "Cousin John" Thrasher's splended hotel served the gentry seeking surcease from the heat.

Roswell was, among other things, the home of Miss Mittie Bulloch, who married President Theodore Roosevelt's father. Bulloch Hall is still a landmark in Roswell.

East Point, an adjoining city which is part of a group known informally as the tri-cities, was the eastern-point junction of Atlanta and West Point railroad with the Macon and Western. It now has 45,000 residents and is the seventh largest city in Georgia.

Hapeville, another of the tri-cities, has 8,500 citizens, is replete with historical markers showing its participation in the destiny of the area, and is a thriving and independent city.

College Park, which began as a 900-acre truck garden, is still another of the tri-cities. It is the home of Woodward Academy—which until 1965 was known as Georgia Military Academy—with alumni all over the world.

Avondale, to the east of Decatur, was the area's first planned community. It still has a great air with its English-village architectural style and cohesiveness of design.

To keep the record straight, Atlanta has had its malodorous sections in the past, and, unhappily, some of them still exist. Others have disappeared, helped by bulldozers and demolition balls. Too many remain.

New retirement and convalescent homes are being built every year to meet varying needs, from medical and hospital care to residential apartments and cottages.

The Peachtree on Peachtree Inn, home for the elderly

Sunny, circular Wesley Woods on Clifton Road N.E. operates 202 residential units for the elderly.

operated by the Georgia Baptist Convention, is smackdab downtown at 175 Peachtree Street N.W. The gift of the Beasley Foundation, it provides 175 modestly priced residential rooms with a common dining room. It has a waiting list.

Wesley Woods, sunny, circular high-rise at 1825 Clifton Road N.E., is Methodist sponsored and it operates 202 residential units, including 40 one-room apartments in its Health Center and Apartment complex. The Health Center is for short-term convalescents, and there is no restriction on age. Residential units are reserved for those sixty-two years old and older.

Canterbury Court, Episcopal-oriented, 3750 Peachtree Road N.E., is a handsome nine-story apartment house with 124 suites, with full dining, library, recreational, chapel and other facilities. Its infirmary serves the needs of its residents under special arrangements made when the apartments are engaged.

With more than 40 major manufacturers of mobile homes, Georgia is the second largest producer of these homes in the nation. Greater Atlanta has at least 140 mobile home parks scattered throughout the city and its environs.

Specific information may be obtained from the Greater Atlanta Mobile Home Association, P. O. Box 686, Hapeville, Georgia 30054.

City, county and state real-estate and personal-property taxes must be filed by April 1 of each year. Returns are based on property owned as of January 1. Call the Tax Receiver's office in the county in which you live, or propose to live, for more specific information.

Out-of-state driver's licenses are valid for 30 days in Georgia. When you apply for a Georgia license, take your birth certificate and from $1.50 to $5 cash to the Driver's License Bureau, 959 Confederate Avenue S. E. Patrol stations in the five counties of metropolitan Atlanta provide this service, but their office hours are less regular.

Georgia license tags must be purchased within 30 days of the time you establish residency. The ad valorem tax on your car must be paid at the time you purchase your tag, and you will need proof of ownership. Take cash, money order or a certified check to the county courthouse to perform this function.

Georgia's motor-vehicle inspection law requires passenger cars to be checked for safety once a year. The cost is $1.25. This inspection can be done at any of the state-designated stations, and any gasoline station can direct you to one.

You may register to vote at 17½ years of age and vote

at 18, after you have lived in Georgia one year, and in the county six months. You may get more voting information from the Registrar's Office in the county in which you live.

In the area of household utilities, call the Georgia Power Company for electricity, Atlanta Gas Light Company for natural gas, the Southern Bell Telephone and Telegraph Company for telephone service, and your own county's water department for water.

Entering children in school will be explained in the next chapter.

During dogwood time Atlanta's streets are lined with blossoms like these in the Lullwater section.

Schools and Colleges

ATLANTA'S EDUCATIONAL establishment is probably the strongest influence in Georgia. Its universities and colleges draw benevolence amounting to millions from private fortunes and pour millions back into the economy through payrolls, research grants and physical expansion.

Its graduates lead in medicine, law, engineering, theology, science, education, the arts and the humanities.

There are 22 degree-granting institutions in Atlanta, four junior colleges, 13 technical schools and 13 business schools, most of them with expanding plants and programs.

Of these, Georgia Institute of Technology, Emory University, the Atlanta University complex and Georgia State College are the largest and most influential.

Georgia Institute of Technology, a unit of the system of the University of Georgia, has long been recognized as one of the nation's leading engineering schools. It has an undergraduate enrollment of approximately 7,500 in day school, another 5,000 or so in night classes, and a graduate school of 1,000 offering master's degrees in 24 fields and doctorates in 11.

The nuclear reactor, second only to M.I.T.'s facility, is the key facility in the Frank H. Neely Nuclear Research

Center at Tech, an expanding department that includes studies into solid-state physics, neutron-defraction chemistry, radiation chemistry, radiobiology, nuclear medicine, reactor kinetics and reactor-engineering problems which involve heat transfer and fluid mechanics.

The great expansion going on everywhere in Atlanta is reflected in Tech's breaking out of its downtown campus. The school has been encircled by a growing city's smothering embrace. It will now grow west and northwest, relocating city traffic arteries and adding 120 acres to its campus in a master plan projected into 1985. By that time, Tech will have a student body of 13,000 in its undergraduate classes alone.

Emory University, which began as the Georgia Conference Manual Labor School in Covington, Georgia, in 1835, is the oldest institution of higher education in Atlanta.

With strong backing from the Candler and Woodruff families, Emory has grown steadily to its present composition of the College of Arts and Sciences, Graduate School and professional schools of Business Administration, Law, Medicine, Theology, Dentistry and Nursing.

Under the spirited leadership of Dr. Sanford Atwood, Emory now has a student body of around 6,000, personnel of 6,600, and an annual budget of almost $49 million. It has just completed a $34 million capital funds program to finance an ambitious new graduate and professional curriculum under its Merit Program.

Georgia State College, which only a few years ago occupied a six-story garage in downtown Atlanta, now has a student body of 6,000, occupies five large buildings with three more under construction. By 1975 it will have transformed its neighborhood, only four blocks from Five Points, into a city university for 25,000 students on a 44-acre platform campus, raised above the level of street traffic.

This is far more than a dream. The Georgia State plan is incorporated into the city's urban-renewal program for the heart of the city. First components of Georgia State's split-level school may already be seen.

Circular staircase at Emory University with bust of benefactor Judge John S. Candler, at left

Dana Fine Arts Building at Agnes Scott College in Decatur

Georgia State and Georgia Tech are state-supported schools, supplemented by their own alumni foundations, but Georgia Tech also receives support from a unique state-wide force. The Joint Tech-Georgia Development Fund, organized in 1955, has raised thousands of dollars annually to reinforce faculty salaries at Georgia Tech and the University of Georgia.

Foremost women's college in the region is Agnes Scott College in Decatur, a Christian liberal arts college of highest academic requirements. It is in its 81st year, with a student body of just under 800 girls and a faculty of close to 100.

Agnes Scott has a master plan for growth and expansion projected into the remainder of the century, which will approximately double its present physical facilities.

A strong phalanx of six independent and church-related colleges and universities, now affiliated in the Atlanta University Center, is the impressive outgrowth of the first humble schools for Negroes established here immediately after the Civil War.

The well-prepared men and women of these colleges are effectively integrated into Atlanta's civic and cultural life. Graduates of Atlanta University's schools are also doing important work throughout the nation.

These schools have benefitted greatly from gifts from the Rockefeller family. They now own collectively 145 acres on the near West Side and have plans to expand into another 80-acre area.

Clark College with 1,033 students, Morehouse with 1,026, Morris Brown with 1,230, Spelman with 850, the Inter-denominational Theological Center with 100 and Atlanta University with 1,065 make joint use of libraries, laboratories, auditoriums and other physical facilities, as well as interchanging teachers and equipment.

Clark and Morris Brown are coeducational liberal arts schools; Morehouse is a liberal arts college for men; and Spelman is the oldest liberal arts college for Negro women in the United States. The Theological Center serves both men and women. Atlanta University is the graduate school for the center.

The Atlanta University Center collectively uses 86 buildings, has 350 full-time faculty members, students from 36 foreign countries, represents $33 million in plant value, another $30 million in endowments and has an annual operating budget of $10 million.

Oglethorpe College, a privately controlled liberal arts college for men and women, has had an interesting history dating back to 1835 when it was begun with a prayer meeting in Milledgeville, Georgia.

Oglethorpe now has a student body of 1,200 and offers B.S. and B.A. degrees, with evening classes for students working toward degrees in Business Administration and Education.

The newest college in the area is Atlanta Baptist College, which opened in September 1968 on a new campus at the Northeast Expressway and Chamblee-Tucker Road, with a plant of four buildings on a 562-acre plot and an initial investment of $7 million.

The new college, connected with the Atlanta Baptist Association, will be operated by its own separate corporation. It will be a coeducational liberal arts undergraduate school with a freshman class of 500 day students.

Atlanta Baptist is the first new four-year college established in this area since the early 1900s, when Georgia State College had its beginning. Dr. Monroe F. Swilley is its first president.

The college-oriented research picture in Georgia, particularly in the biotechnical fields, is broad and growing broader. Atlanta is especially well-equipped with resources and talents to make great scientific advances. There are:

Morehouse College, part of Atlanta University complex in downtown Atlanta

the nuclear reactor and computer center at Georgia Tech, Emory University with its health research, its complex of hospitals engaged in clinical research, the Yerkes Primate Laboratory, the U.S. Public Health Service's Communicable Disease Center. All are reinforced by the facilities of colleges and universities of the state and region.

Several hundred scientists, most of them holding doctoral degrees, are at work at medical, biological, nuclear, agricultural and engineering research projects. Many installations are in progress at Georgia Tech, Emory, Georgia State, Atlanta University, Agnes Scott College, University of Georgia, Grady Hospital, St. Joseph's Infirmary and Piedmont Hospital, Georgia Department of Public Health, Georgia Mental Health Institute, Southeastern Water Laboratory, the Communicable Disease Center, and Lockheed-Georgia Company.

The Atlanta area has six junior colleges, two of them less than five years old.

DeKalb College, 555 North Indian Creek Drive, Clarkston, is operated with state aid by the DeKalb County Board of Education. It was opened in 1964 and within three years had a student body of more than 3,000, all working toward junior college diplomas in the liberal arts.

Newest two-year institution is Kennesaw Junior College, a unit of the University System of Georgia. It opened in September 1966, and within one year had a student body of more than 1,000 with courses leading to Associate in Science and Arts.

Southern Technical Institute, Marietta, a unit of the Engineering Extension Division of Georgia Tech, offers evening and day courses leading to associate engineering degrees. It is a two-year technical school. Credit from its specialized courses, however, cannot be applied to senior college work.

The Marietta Center, off-campus center for the University of Georgia, offers courses leading to degrees at the University at Athens.

John Marshall University, 105 Forrest Avenue N. E., is a private coeducational day and evening junior college and law school which offers degrees and certificate of Associate in Arts and Business Administration, with concentration on either management or secretarial sciences.

Massey Junior College, Marietta at Forsyth Streets, is a business-skills-oriented school, which also includes a law school. Its merchandising division includes the Fashion Institute of America, which operates its own retailing shop.

Many private business, career and professional schools and colleges offer courses. Some of these lead to degrees. They include:

The Alliance Française French School   50 Whitehall St. S.W.

The Atlanta School of Art   Atlanta Memorial Arts Center, Peachtree at 15th St—Bachelor of Fine Arts in graphic design, painting, sculpture and printmaking

Atlanta Christian College   2605 Ben Hill Dr., East Point
Bachelor of arts in Religion

Atlanta Law School   106 Forsyth St. N.W.
Bachelor and Master of Laws

The Berlitz School of Languages   3400 Peachtree Rd. N.E.

Cashier's Training Institute   66 Luckie St. N.W.
business skills

Columbia Theological Seminary   701 Columbia Dr., Decatur
Bachelor of Religion, Master in Christian Education, Biblical, Historical, Systematic and Pastoral Theology

Immanuel College   644 Memorial Dr. S.E.
Bachelor of Arts in theology, religious education; Master of Arts in religious education

Interdenominational Theological Center   671 Beckwith St. S.W.
Bachelor of Divinity, Master of Religious Education, Sacred Theology

Mercer University Southern College of Pharmacy 223 Waltona
St. N.W.

Bachelor of Science in pharmacy. (New school already begun
in DeKalb County on Indian Creek Road.)

There are many other special schools, a listing of which
may be found in the Yellow Pages of the telephone book.

Undergirding all of this are the elementary, secondary
public and private school systems and the vocational institutions of the region.

The educational complex of metropolitan Atlanta now
has nine school systems. Every school is accredited by the
Georgia Accrediting Commission. Each of the high schools
has earned the highest certification possible, that of the
Southern Association of Colleges and Secondary Schools.

Statistics change every season, but as this goes to press,
the total enrollment in the Atlanta public school system,
which is headed by Dr. John W. Letson, Superintendent,
hovers around 120,000, including 119 elementary schools,
25 high schools, one middle school, 12 special schools, two
night schools and one area technical school with day and
night student bodies.

A long-range study has been under way for several years
looking toward the possible merger of the Atlanta public
schools with the Fulton County system of 52 elementary
and 15 senior high schools.

For specific information about schools in any particular
area, you may telephone:

City of Atlanta	522-3381
Fulton County	572-2161
Cobb County	422-3471
Clayton County	478-9991
City of Decatur	474-5344
DeKalb County	371-2407
City of Marietta	422-3500
Gwinnett County	963-9248

Thirty-one private schools in the region also provide diverse facilities and services. Five of these accept pupils from kindergarten through the twelfth grade. They include:

Lovett School   4075 Paces Ferry Rd. N.W.

Pace Academy   966 West Paces Ferry Rd. N.W.

Arlington Schools   2605 Fairburn Rd. S.W.

Trinity Schools of the South   3003 Howell Mill Rd. N.W.

Westminister School for Boys and *Westminister School for Girls*   1424 West Paces Ferry Rd. N.W.

The following are private high schools:

Woodward Academy   P.O. Box 119, College Park

Immanuel Christian High School   644 Memorial Dr. S.E.

D'Youville Academy for Girls   4144 Chamblee-Dunwoody Rd., Chamblee

Marist College   3790 Ashford Dunwoody Rd. N.E.

Saint Pius X   2674 Johnson Rd. N.E.

St. Joseph's   320 Courtland St. N.E.

Drexel Catholic   631 Harwell Rd. N.W.

Seven private schools offer only the elementary grades:

Ar'Lyn Worth School   1463 Oxford Rd. N.E.

Colonial Hill Christian Schools   2134 Newnan Ave., East Point

Grace Christian School   2609 Memorial Dr. S.E.

The Hebrew Academy of Atlanta   1140 University Dr. N.E.

Happyland School   995 St. Charles Ave. N.E.

Trinity School   3003 Howell Mill Rd. N.W.

Holy Innocents Day School   805 Mt. Vernon Highway N.W.

The following schools use the Maria Montessori methods and techniques:

Ashdun Hall   3830 Ashford Dunwoody Rd. N.E.

First Montessori   3725 Powers Ferry Rd. N.W.

Second Montessori   St. Anne's Episcopal Church, 3098 Rilman Rd. N.W.

Flat Shoals Montessori   2780 Flat Shoals Rd., Decatur

Pebble Brook Montessori   5500 Winter Chapel Rd., Doraville

Early Learning Center   3359 Peachtree Rd. N.E.

Stratford Schools   2528 Chamblee Tucker Rd., Doraville

Marietta Montessori Schools   Marietta

For children with special needs, the City of Atlanta, Fulton, Cobb, DeKalb and Gwinnett counties provide special public schools. A telephone call to the Special Education departments of these systems will give precise details on the varying programs.

There are eight other schools for handicapped children; these are classified as private, but some receive grants from public school systems for whom they take children under special referral:

Atlanta Speech School   3160 Northside Parkway N.W.

Cerebral Palsy Center of Atlanta   1815 Ponce de Leon Ave. N.W.

Creswell School   101 Delmar Rd., Marietta

Fairhaven School   833 Springdale Rd. N.E.

Little Red School   with branches at 1595 and 302 East Vesta Ave., College Park

Marian Howard School   1790 La Vista Rd. N.E.

The Northside School   3166 Mathieson Dr. N.E.

Our Lady's Day School   631 Harwell Rd. N.W.

Five private schools give special training for normal children who need remedial teaching:

Appleton   43 Third St. N.E.

Brandon Hall   Spalding Dr., Dunwoody
The Hinman School   293 Pharr Rd. N.E.
The Oxford School   3908 Peachtree Rd. N.E.
The Reading Center   3511 Piedmont Rd. N.E.

Thirteen public and private vocational schools train workers for the business and industrial community.

Of these, the Atlanta Area Technical School, 1560 Stewart Avenue S.W., is the newest and largest, serving both Atlanta and Fulton County with courses not offered by any other school in the state. Among its 42 instructional areas are Construction, Instrumentation, Sanitary Engineering, Commercial Food Service.

Atlanta Tech, an $8 million school, is one of 25 such public institutions established in Georgia recently. It covers the area of seven football fields, is open to anyone over 16 years of age who is not enrolled in school. Eighty percent of its students are high school graduates and adults seeking retraining in new technological skills.

This school and four others are public, tuition-free schools, designed for adult education in vocational fields: DeKalb Area Technical School, the Marietta Cobb Area Vocational Technical School, Hoke Smith Technical School and Carver Vocational High School.

Hoke Smith, South Expressway and Stewart Avenue, operates public day and night schools in a completely equipped, newly renovated location with provisions for 10,000 students.

Fernbank Science Center, mentioned in an early tour of the city, is a science complex unlike anything else in the Southeast.

In addition to its impressive planetarium, laboratory and observatory, it has recently received a Telstar Satellite valued at more than $1 million. On loan from the Southern Bell Telephone Company, this satellite was built as a back-up for the satellite now in operation 3,600 miles from the earth.

Fernbank is owned by the DeKalb Board of Education, but its facilities are available to students of Emory, Agnes Scott and DeKalb Colleges, as well as public schools of Atlanta and adjacent counties.

Lupton Hall of Oglethorpe College in North Atlanta. The school was named for the founder of Georgia, the 13th colony.

Churches

"I'M FIGHTING the devil and will fight him as long as there is anything to fight with. I will fight him with my hands. I will fight him with my feet. I will bite him until there is not a tooth in my head. When my teeth are gone, I'll gum him until I die. . . ."

These were the words of Sam P. Jones, the great evangelist of 1900, shouting a defiance that was repeated by Wiliam Ashley (Billy) Sunday 17 years later when he opened a strenuous campaign against his satanic majesty in an old circus grounds at the Jackson Street Tabernacle in Atlanta.

"O God," pleaded Billy, "if this city of Atlanta, this pearl of the South, will fall on her knees before you, then I say that the whole Southland, drenched in the tears of repentance, will do as Atlanta does. . . ."

A host of men have fought the devil in this pearl of the South since the city began, many of them losing the fight. But the churches of the city, which catalyzed the fervor of a lusty people in the early days, still galvanize their descendants with standing room only at most services.

Greater Atlanta has 1,500 churches with a total membership of 745,000. The city proper has 650 churches, representing 40 creeds. They range from the most austerely restrained denominations to the most informal communions, embracing holy water at the fount and humble footwashing at the altar, rituals and regalia, the bread and wine of sacraments, the raising of maces, the lighting of candles, the handling of deadly snakes. They invite dialogues, art exhibits, book reviews, hippie dramas.

The worship includes music of contrapuntal antiquity, the majestic chants of the orthodox, the celebration of trumpets and violins, the full-throated sound of mighty organs. It includes the voices of operatic prima donnas, children, housewives and the moving counterpoint of Negro choirs.

The church here, as elsewhere, has ever been at the crossroads.

It is a pallid week that does not find some group, lay or ordained, descrying ivory towers and arguing the function of the contemporary church.

But churches are wherever the action is. Indeed, as gadflies, they inspire much of the action. They preach, teach, sweat, work, operate kindergartens, build colleges, struggle with bitter souls, drug addicts, alcoholics, criminals and the poor. They seek out the "night people," build shelters for the elderly, minister to babies, care for the sick, operate missions, argue war and peace, counsel the mentally disturbed, rootless and disenchanted. They deal with the up-and-out as well as the down-and-out, and they eternally confront the smug.

Many of the towering figures of Atlanta wear or have worn the garb of religious commitment, including the late Roman Catholic Archbishop Paul J. Hallinan, who during his last years in Atlanta ironically occupied the former headquarters of the Grand Dragon of the Ku Klux Klan, and the late Dr. Martin Luther King, Jr., martyred middleman of social revolution.

With the Rev. William Holmes Borders in the pulpit, the Wheat Street Baptist Church underwrote the first Negro-

Big Bethel African Methodist Episcopal Church on Auburn Avenue, where "Heaven Bound" plays

sponsored rental-housing project of its kind in the nation. With considerable cooperation from other local leaders, the church built a 500-apartment three-story garden-type complex in the Butler Street Urban Renewal area. A nonprofit, low-interest project, it cost almost $3,000,000 and was constructed by a local Negro contracting firm.

One of the progressive forces of the religious community is the Atlanta Council of Churchwomen, whose ecumenical efforts have affected social conditions here since 1928. An interdenominational membership of some 600 activists, these women work with youth and also in the areas of health, race, criminal rehabilitation or wherever need or support seems indicated.

For the breadth of its work, the organization won the national Lane Bryant Award for Civic Service in the 1950s.

The Fellowship of Christian Athletes, a national organization, has its Southeastern regional headquarters here at 2658 Cove Circle N.E. In this sports-conscious community, practically every coach, athlete and institution, as well as hundreds of laymen, supports and participates in this fellowship movement.

In addition to mission work extensively undertaken by the Salvation Army and other smaller community missions for teaching, rehabilitation or both, the Atlanta Union Mission, 54 Ellis Street, is one of the largest missions in the nation. Nondenominational, it receives support from many churches, civic clubs and the general public in its service to homeless men, which includes medical treatment and an infirmary. The Atlanta Union Mission has been in operation continuously since 1942.

Names of specific churches may be found in the Yellow Pages of the telephone book, divided into denominations. Services and sermon titles are carried in the Saturday editions of the Atlanta Constitution and the Atlanta Journal.

Almost every church has its particular attraction. For special interests, we suggest visits to the following:

THE CATHEDRAL OF ST. PHILIP (*Episcopalian*) 2744

Peachtree Rd. N.W.: For its Gothic authority, its seven altar accessories in contemporary design by Julian Hoke Harris; its great rose window transepts, apsidal and aisle windows from Willet Studios, and for altar rail and kneelers in the exquisite needlework designs of women communicants.

THE CATHEDRAL OF CHRIST THE KING (*Roman Catholic*) 2699 Peachtree Rd. N.E.: For its stained-glass windows, especially the rose window over the main altar reminiscent of a similar window at Chartres Cathedral, the others showing Old Testament figures, Columbus' arrival in the new world, history of the church in Georgia, and the coat of arms of Archbishop O'Hara, who was Bishop of Atlanta and Savannah when this cathedral was built. The windows are all by Willet Studios.

SECOND PONCE DE LEON CHURCH (*Baptist*) 2715 Peachtree Rd. N.E.: For the quiet purity of its sanctuary and the use of virtuoso instrumental music in its worship.

AHAVATH ACHIM SYNAGOGUE (*Conservative Jewish*) Peachtree Battle and Northside Dr.: For the Ellman chapel windows, Menorah, eternal light and art doors of the synagogue, all manufactured to designs of Perli Pelzig by Llorens Studios of Atlanta. Visitors: Sunday to Friday, 9 A.M.–5 P.M.

GREEK ORTHODOX CHURCH OF THE ANNUNCIATION 2500 Clairmont Road, N.E.: For its spectacular Byzantine architecture and the splendid mosaic ikons by Sirio Tenelli of Italy.

THE IMMACULATE HEART OF MARY CHURCH (*Roman Catholic*) 2855 Briarcliff Rd. N.E.: For the stations of the cross and stylized terra cotta Madonna over the outside entrance, sculpture of Julian Hoke Harris: for the Annunciation painting in the left chapel by George Beattie.

THE TEMPLE (*Reform Jewish*) 1589 Peachtree N.E.: For its paintings by George Beattie, Mexico's Leonardo Nierman, Israel's Reuben Rubin, and for the significant plaque in the new Social Hall: "How pleasant it is for brothers to dwell together in unity . . . in gratitude to those whose comfort and encouragement sustained and

The Temple (Reform Jewish) contains paintings by noted artists George Beattie of Atlanta, Mexico's Leonardo Nierman and Israel's Reuben Rubin.

strengthened us, we dedicate this as Friendship Hall." This plaque is a reminder that in 1958 the Temple, the house of worship of this congregation with more than a hundred year's history in Atlanta, was bombed by terrorists from another state. There was overwhelming sympathetic response to the congregation from the Atlanta community and an insistence on participation in the rebuilding of the Temple.

UNITARIAN-UNIVERSALIST CONGREGATION OF ATLANTA 1911 Cliff Valley Rd. N.E.: For the design of its circular sanctuary, fashioned after a theater in the round; for its gallery of changing exhibits of paintings and sculpture; for its use of art forms replacing stained glass windows and statuary.

THE CHAPEL AT YOUNG WOMEN'S CHRISTIAN ASSOCIATION 72 Edgewood Ave. N.E.: For its exquisite small chapel, the graceful gift to young women who have come to Atlanta for work or education, from the late Mrs. Howard C. Candler.

DRUID HILLS PRESBYTERIAN CHURCH 1026 Ponce de Leon Ave. N.E.: For its aisle, chancel and small rose windows in the west gallery by Willet Studios.

ST. MARK'S METHODIST CHURCH 781 Peachtree St. N.E.: For the music of its choirs led by Dr. Michael McDowell.

ST. LUKE'S EPISCOPAL CHURCH 435 Peachtree St. N.E.: For its stained-glass windows and for its choir directed by Minister of Music Hugh Hodgson, as well as for his exalted playing of the organ.

LUTHERAN CHURCH OF THE ASCENSION 4000 Roswell Rd. N.E.: For its Ascending Christ, carved of elmwood by Otto Flath.

LUTHERAN CHURCH OF THE REDEEMER 731 Peachtree St. N.E.: For its graceful architecture, the clerestory and sanctuary windows and illuminated cross in the west façade by Willet Studios.

PEACHTREE CHRISTIAN CHURCH 1580 Peachtree Rd. N.W.: For its aisle windows, "Parable of the Prodigal Son," by H. Vernon Spreadbury of England, also the window of Christ's Blessing, by Rambusch Studios.

METHODIST CENTER 159 Forrest Ave. N.E.: For its stained-glass history of Christianity and Methodism, manufactured in London in the 1800s, its 12,000 pieces restored and installed here by Llorens Studio.

FIRST PRESBYTERIAN CHURCH 1328 Peachtree St. N.E.: For its red granite "Jet "madonna, worked with flame but without chisel or abrasive by Julian Hoke Harris.

EBENEZER BAPTIST CHURCH 413 Auburn Ave. N.E.: Where Martin Luther King, Sr., and his son, Martin Luther King, Jr., were pastor and co-pastor until the latter's assassination in Memphis.

Clubs and Organizations

I T H A S always been easy to round up a quorum in Atlanta.

Starting with Humbug Square in 1855, where snake-oil men, fakirs, itinerant evangelists, banjo pickers and pitchmen drew their kind, people here have figured if it's fun doing, it's more fun doing it with someone else.

Atlanta has groups to which potential members must bring a heritage and a pedigree. It also has the old Burns Club, in existence since 1896 and organized by "Jews, Gentiles, Catholics, Protestants, College Professors, Judges, Capitalists, Stonecutters, the Lettered and the Unlettered."

The Burns Club has its own wee cottage at 988 Alloway Place S.W., with a butt, ben, byre and barm exactly like the poet's birthplace in Auld Scotland.

Atlanta has pipe smokers clubs, old maids clubs, clubs for single adults, married adults, divorced adults, widowed men and women. The city has all the Anonymous family, including Neurotics Anonymous. Even the Boneheads have an organization.

There are skating clubs, sports-car clubs, gymnkhanas, judo clubs, karate funsters, air-travel groups.

If you are looking for something special, ask your neighbor if he's a member of whatever it is and see if that leads you there. Churches usually know about offbeat aggregations too, as well as the religious and faith societies that have been meeting regularly here since the first hands were folded in public prayer.

If, after a few weeks' investigation, you still do not find an existing cadre concentrating on your particular interest, the best thing to do is start a club yourself. It will be an instant success.

Society in Atlanta has no countable Four Hundred. It has concentric circles that tighten or expand depending upon the occasion, the situation, or the pressure.

The city has cafes, cabarets and rendezvous uncounted, but Atlanta has no cafe society in the sense that this exists in such cities as New York. No gossip columnists notice who is where, with whom or why. The only time guests are acknowledged anywhere in public print is when the sponsors of the event involved ask for special attention.

Sets exist from Sedate to Rocket, gardes from Old to Avant, each of them doing their thing with the companions of their choice. The choice may be old buddies known since childhood, since college, since a promotion at the office or since yesterday.

Entertainment at the personal level centers around private clubs, private drawing rooms or private swimming pools. Attire may be white tie or paper party pack—it all depends.

For great civic works, a few powerful people are required. No one confuses them with anyone else. Their names, like that of Abou ben Adhem, are writ large upon Atlanta's Book of Gold. Their tribe doth increase.

Being to the manor born is its own reward here as elsewhere, but flair, taste, and charm never go unnoticed even in our heterogeneous society.

Cynics have noted that social acceptance of a sort may be bought at a price and that the moneyed path is the big charity route. As with other cities in the nation, we have our gala charity balls for which one pays one's way with a precalculated offering, but it must be said that engraved invitations are not wasted on more prospects than might be comfortably seated at supper tables, should they accept.

The patronage habit draws instant appreciation and attention. Sizable checks to fund campaigns of any type bear a certain eclat of their own. They lead to instant welcome in many groups.

Aside from private homes, the city's exclusive social and recreational life centers around its private men's clubs. Membership, by selective invitation only, proceeds through the male head of the household. Use of club facilities may be passed on through inheritance to unmarried daughters and left as legacies to widows for their lifetimes.

Oldest of these organizations are the Capital City Club and the Piedmont Driving Club. They rank equally as settings for elegant and important society functions, with much of their membership overlapping.

The Capital City Club grew out of a meeting in 1883 of four young men in search of a place to play billiards. The club now has a country installation at Brookhaven with an 18-hole golf course, a lake, swimming, tennis, health and dining facilities, and a city club at 7 Harris Street with full club entertainment facilities.

The Piedmont Driving Club evolved from the Gentlemen's Driving Club organized in 1887 by sportsmen for driving and racing their fine horses "in grounds where the wives and children of members might be taken without fear of mingling with improper characters."

From that day to this, no improper characters have ever been identified mingling at the Driving Club, but a great many stunningly gowned daughters of the well-to-do have made their bows there to society, and many a dignitary of utmost importance has been received with appropriate ceremony.

The Jewish social life of the community has revolved around the Standard Club which grew out of the Concordia

Club founded in 1867. The Standard Club's latest fine club-house and golf course is on Standard Road, on the north side of the city.

The Atlanta Athletic Club is Atlanta's largest club, perhaps the largest in the southeast. In addition to a yacht club at Lake Lanier and a golf course to the north, its downtown Atlanta headquarters has extensive club facilities and sixty bedrooms, many of which are occupied by resident members on a permanent basis.

Two other private clubs deserve special mention. The Commerce Club is the closest thing in Atlanta to a British gentlemen's club. It's an all-male luncheon sanctuary in the Commerce Building where executives can get away from it all, including wives. Sumptuous antebellum-mansion grandeur pervades the two floors connected with a magnificent curving stairway. Facilities include an oak-paneled bar, card rooms, reading rooms, dining rooms—far too handsome for digs where women are cheerfully excluded.

The Cherokee Club, organized in the mid-1950s, is popular and growing in its facilities. The town club is on the old Grant estate on West Paces Ferry. Cherokee's golf course is on Hightower Trail, a mile or so from Roswell, bordering the Chattahoochee River.

There are many clubs of importance, each of them with special pleaders, including several yacht clubs awash with aquatic ardor, especially on weekends:

Ansley Golf and Country Club   196 Montgomery Ferry Dr. N.E.

Allatoona Yacht Club   Lake Allatoona

Atlanta Athletic Club   166 Carnegie Way N.W.

Atlanta Yacht Club   Lake Lanier

Capital City Club   7 Harris St. N.W.

Chattahoochee Plantation Club   531 Paper Mill Rd. S.E., Marietta

Cherokee Town and Country Club   155 West Paces Ferry Rd. N.W.

The Commerce Club   Commerce Bldg.
Druid Hills Golf Club   740 Clifton Rd. N.E.
East Lake Country Club   East Lake, Decatur
Flat Creek Golf Club   Peachtree City
Lake Lanier Sailing Club   Lake Lanier
Lanier Yacht Club   Lake Lanier
Lakeside Country Club   3600 Old Fairburn Rd. S.W.
New Lincoln Country Club   2405 Simpson Rd. N.W.
Peachtree Golf Club   4800 Peachtree Rd. N.W.
Piedmont Driving Club   1215 Piedmont Ave. N.E.
Progressive Club   1050 Techwood Dr. N.W.
River Bend Club   Highway 141, Norcross
Standard Club   Standard Dr., Brookhaven
University Yacht Club   Lake Lanier

All the major men's luncheon clubs have one or more affiliates here. The Rotary Club, oldest of the men's luncheon clubs in Atlanta, was established in 1913 in what had once been the law offices of Woodrow Wilson.

The Atlanta Junior Chamber of Commerce has for 40 years conducted the annual Empty Stocking campaign at Christmas time to raise money for giftless children. With great verve, the Jaycees ring doorbells and stop motorists at street corners to sell the Empty Stocking edition of the *Atlanta Journal and Constitution*, always with resounding success. Of course the Jaycees have other projects, but this one is closest to the hearts of the public.

The fourth largest Junior League in the United States works effectively in Atlanta. The city's top young society women were organized here 53 years ago for community service and they have since been active in every phase of life—health, education, child care, the arts, legal aid—but their special project was the establishment and nurturing of the city's outstanding Atlanta Speech School.

Decatur, Marietta and College Park have Junior Service Leagues, whose purpose is similar to that of the Atlanta Junior League, each with its own projects.

B'nai B'rith has its regional and district headquarters here, as well as groups throughout the city, and there are active chapters of the National Council of Jewish Women and of Hadassah, which operates its own fund-raising bargain store.

Atlanta is the regional headquarters for U.S.O., which operates an information center at 151 Spring Street N.W.

The Atlanta Committee for Foreign Visitors, 615 Peachtree Street N.E., is a quasi-official organization. It welcomes hundreds of visitors from other lands each year, aiding them in their various quests for information and arranging compatible hospitality with local families when it is desired. Volunteer hosts are always welcome to register with the committee.

More than 500 garden clubs of varying special interests abound in the territory, including several for men. Men also participate in others on a coeducational basis.

Most of the green-thumbers have scheduled programs throughout the year, except in July and August. Most participate in six or seven annual flower shows: Daffodil in March, Tulip in April, Iris in May, Rose in May, Hemerocallis in June, the Symphony Flower Show in September, and Chrysanthemum in October.

Since 1934, Rich's, as a public service, has provided quarters and staff in its downtown store for a Garden Center for the area. Two hundred and thirty seven clubs belong to the Center and participate in continuous competitive displays of artistic arrangements and horticultural exhibits.

The Atlanta Writers Club was organized in 1914 to lend help and encouragement to local literary talent. It still exists for the same purpose.

The Atlanta League of Women Voters is one of the most influential and respected nonpartisan political forces in the community.

Here, as elsewhere, women are organized in community clubs with civic, philanthropic, legislative and social purposes.

The oldest of such organizations in Atlanta is the Atlanta Woman's Club, chartered in 1896. Its headquarters is now in a fine old stone residence on Peachtree Street at 14th Street, where it also operates the Community Playhouse, a small and tasteful theater.

The largest women's clubs are united under the umbrella of the Georgia Federation of Women's Clubs. The Georgia Federation owns and operates the Tallulah Falls School, a grammar and high school in north Georgia, the only Federated Club organization in the nation to undertake such a commitment.

Many professional women's clubs exist here, including the Business and Professional Women's Club, with several chapters. Its headquarters are at 61 Eighth Street N.E.

Several musical groups are open to general membership. For a membership fee of $10 any woman may become a member of the Women's Association of the Atlanta Symphony and may work actively in any of several areas or simply take a passive role as a contributing supporter. The Atlanta Music Club and the Atlanta Opera Council invite supporting memberships.

The Jewish Community Center, 1745 Peachtree Street N.E., carries on an extensive program in its large center for persons of all ages, including day and resident summer camps, organized services for children, adults and golden agers.

Volunteering is big business in Atlanta. Opportunities exist where interests lie.

All the city's hospitals seek aides in one area of service or another.

In its annual fund drive, the United Appeal represents a group of 45 service organizations. The United Appeal campaign welcomes serious volunteers, and each of the agencies it represents invites continuing or special volunteer help for its own particular needs.

Among United Appeal agencies are those serving persons of all ages and conditions, from Campfire Girls and

Boy and Girl Scouts through the interests and welfare of retired and elderly people.

The health agencies not included in the United Appeal always seek volunteer aides. They include such research and clinical forces as The National Foundation, the American Cancer Society, the National Heart Association and others of this type.

All the arts, visual and performing, beseech the understanding support of talented volunteers. Tickets for all performances, except those restricted to members, are always offered to the public.

One of the favorite preoccupations of Atlantans is house touring, a curiosity that pays off handsomely for various groups which organize public invasions of impressive private homes and gardens for the price of a ticket or contribution to their good works.

Watch the social sections of the daily newspapers for these announcements. House tours usually occur in the spring, when gardens are at their glorious peak, giving strangers an opportunity to inspect with impunity some of the best residential architecture and landscaping and the most tasteful furnishings and appointments.

There are college alumni chapters, professional associations, coin- and stamp-collecting groups, an English-Speaking Union and an Alliance Française. The Alliance maintains its own French language school at 50 Whitehall Street S.W.

The news and information media have their Atlanta Press Club.

The Atlanta Chapter of the National Railway Historical Society has its Southeastern Railway Museum at Lakewood Park with a film library and 21 rolling pieces, including several beautiful old iron pets they call by such names as "Maud," "Old 304," and "Old 750." These are steam locomotives.

A new group called the Georgia Conservancy is at work here visiting and appreciating historic areas and guarding nature preserves. There are also bird watchers, both organized and unorganized.

If none of these groups appeals, and life still seems empty and jaded, there are always the introduction corporations, which seem to do a Gretna Green office business in this community with 300,000 single adults in residence. This guidebook cannot attempt to list these services. In the Cupid business, who could compete with a computer?

National Communicable Disease Center on Clifton Rd. N.E. near Emory University conducts worldwide medical program.

Hospitals and Medical Research

I F S O D A water, aspirin and a good night's rest won't cure you, there are 23 general and ten special hospitals to turn to. One of these is named for Crawford W. Long, the Georgia surgeon who first successfully used anesthesia in an operation.

Depending upon how old you are, the hospitals have a bed and bassinet capacity of almost 5,000. Five more general hospitals are under way with 1,000 more beds.

Atlanta is the medical center of the South with 1,700 physicians, 527 dentists, and extensive hospital, research and educational facilities. There are more than 4,500 registered and practical nurses to soothe your brow.

Atlanta is headquarters for the Southeastern region of the United States Public Health Service and national headquarters for its Communicable Disease Center. Hundreds of scientists and laboratory technicians are at work here to conquer all communicable diseases from pertussis to tuberculosis. They even do research on ways to protect earthlings from stray ailments that astronauts might pick up in other spheres.

The Communicable Disease Center employs more than 100 specialists in production and distribution of medical films, videotapes, slides, filmstrips and other visual materials. The CDC operates the largest medical motion picture studio in the nation.

Emory University's School of Medicine is one of two medical colleges in Georgia, and with the School of Dentistry has an enrollment of 600 students. Emory is attacking high mortality rates among indigent mothers and babies, developing family planning programs, and studying methods of rehabilitating alcoholics. Under a $2 million Economic Opportunity grant, Emory has set up a model community neighborhood health center, stressing treatment and preventive medicine among needy families. Emory also has a division of nuclear medicine; students are required to study in the nuclear field as well as related physics and biochemistry in other departments.

Six schools of nursing have an enrollment of more than 1,500 students.

Georgia State College opened a new School of Allied Health Sciences in 1968, with degree programs in medical technology, occupational therapy, physical therapy, respiration therapy, radiological technology and nursing.

The Community Tele-Med system, the nation's first community medical-television network, a facility of the U.S. Public Health Service, links the Emory School of Medicine, Emory University Hospital, Grady Memorial Hospital, Veterans Administration Hospital, Georgia Department of Public Health and its Mental Health Institute. It allows two-way visual and aural communications between Grady Hospital and the audiovisual facility.

Atlanta's general hospital, Grady Memorial, is the largest hospital under one roof in the nation. Governed by the Fulton-DeKalb Hospital Authority, it is the principal clinical teaching facility of Emory Medical School.

Georgia Baptist Hospital, owned by the Baptist Convention of Georgia, the second largest hospital in the metropolitan area, has just added a new $6 million wing, which

Grady Memorial Hospital, largest under one roof in the country

will include the Scottish Rite Hospital for Crippled Children in its Center.

Among a number of special hospitals are the Henrietta Egleston Hospital for children and Elks Aidmore Hospital, a rehabilitation and convalescent hospital for children.

The world-famous Cerebral Palsy Center of Atlanta is a showplace, not only for its modern facilities for the treatment of victims of cerebral palsy of all ages, but also because of its beautiful setting atop a landscaped hill with cascading gardens.

Piedmont Hospital is the beneficiary of an annual gala ball, sponsored by its loyal women's auxiliary. The Piedmont Ball is a high point in the winter's social season.

Shopping and Services

FASHIONS IN clothing and household furnishings are always fresh in Atlanta.

Every emporium has its special excellence and its special public.

The large department stores carry complete stocks of merchandise and services in a wide price range, from European original fashions to automobile rentals. They also have complete calendars of entertainment and special events which play to standing-room-only audiences.

The old-time big three of Atlanta are:

Davison's   Main store at 180 Peachtree St. N.E.; branches at Columbia Mall; Lenox Square Shopping Center

Rich's, Inc.   Main store at 45 Broad St. S.W.; branches at Belvedere Plaza, Cobb County, Greenbriar, Lenox Square and North DeKalb Shopping Centers

Sears, Roebuck and Co.   Main store at 677 Ponce de Leon Ave. N.E.; branches at 3060 Peachtree Rd. N.W.; 895 Gordon Rd. S.W.; 3570 Memorial Dr., Decatur; 995 Roswell Rd., Marietta; plus other appliance and mail order centers

The following women's fashion stores carry fine women's apparel, accessories, children's clothing and gifts:

J. P. Allen and Co.   Main store at 214 Peachtree St. N.E.; branches at Lenox Square and Greenbriar Shopping Centers

Franklin Simon   640 Peachtree St. N.E.; Greenbriar and Lenox Square Shopping Centers

Lane Bryant, Inc.   218 Peachtree St. N.W.

Regenstein's   Main store at 209 Peachtree St. N.E.; branches at 3187 Peachtree Rd. N.E.; 2044 Lawrenceville Highway, Decatur

Saks Fifth Avenue   Phipps Plaza (also men's clothing)

Women's specialty shops concentrate on women's apparel, accessories, some gifts:

Joseph Brennan   Lenox Square and 1931A Peachtree Rd. N.E.

Leon Frohsin   230 Peachtree St. N.E.; Lenox Square Shopping Center

Peck and Peck   Lenox Square Shopping Center

Muse's   Henry Grady Hotel and 630 Peachtree St. N.E.

Eugene Weinberg   Lenox Square Shopping Center

For informal leisure-time clothes there are:

Casual Corner   281 E. Paces Ferry Rd. N.E.; 135 Sycamore St., Decatur; North DeKalb and Lenox Square Shopping Centers

Singer's Casual Shop   3699 Roswell Rd. N.W.; 2098 N. Decatur Plaza, Decatur; Lenox Square, Greenbriar, Belvedere and Sandy Springs Shopping Centers

The following men's furnishings stores carry brandname lines of men's clothing and accessories and some gifts:

Baron's   3500 Peachtree Rd. N.W.

Brooks Brothers   145 Peachtree N.W.

Hirsch's   79 Peachtree St. N.E.; Lenox Square, Beleveedere, Cobb County, Greenbriar and North DeKalb Shopping Centers

Christmas tree glows atop glass bridge over Forsyth Street that connects the two stores of Rich's, Inc.

Muse's   52 Peachtree St. N.W.; Greenbriar, Lenox Square Shopping Centers

Parks-Chambers, Inc.   43 Peachtree St. N.E.; Lenox Square and West Paces Ferry Shopping Centers

Spencer's, Ltd.   693 Peachtree St. N.E.

H. Stockton, Inc.   80 Forsyth St.; North DeKalb Shopping Center

Zachry's   87 Peachtree N.E.; Lenox Square, N. DeKalb and Greenbriar Shopping Centers

Most of the shopping centers consider one of their primary roles to be Pied Pipers to the public, especially during seasons preceding holidays. A check of the schedule of events at any shopping center will show upcoming dates featuring hobbies and interests of every variety from performing seals to sports-car rallies. These are almost always free and worth the minutes they take to get there.

Atlanta has dozens of art galleries and antique shops. (Art galleries are listed in the Arts section.) Antique shops, like their wares, are unexpected jewels to be discovered privately. New antique shops spring up like clusters of mushrooms after a rain. This minute, a few blocks from you, there may be a small treasure trove with a burden of priceless loot from the past.

With such an abundance of dazzling plunder, we must leave you to your own instincts. Part of the fun of antiquing is the finding.

Note in passing: Vinings, one settlement a few miles north of Atlanta off to the left of U.S. 41, is practically an heirloom in itself. It has six or seven shops housed separately and several more grouped together in an ancient pavilion built by railroad crews long ago as a dance hall.

Here are a few miscellaneous addresses to tide you over until you discover your own favorite shops:

AUCTION HOUSES:

Atlanta Auction Gallery   1405 Spring St. N.W. and 505 W. Peachtree St. N.E. Auctions: Wednesday and Thursday, 7:30 P.M.

Lenox Square Shopping Center provides enough parking for all. At left is Davison's branch store.

Above parking deck at right is branch store of Rich's, largest in Center.

Books, New:

Baptist Book Store   283 Peachtree St. N.E.
Cokesbury   72 Broad St. N.E.
Davison's   All branches
Elsons   Lenox Square, Greenbriar and Cobb Shopping Centers
Millers   64 Broad St. N.W. and five other locations
Rich's   All branches

Books, out-of-print and historic:

Abrams Books, Inc.   3230 Peachtree Rd. N.W.
Kimsey Book Shop   187 Spring St. N.W.

Butcher Shop:

Alex's Butcher Shop   322 Pharr Rd. N.E.

Cakes:

Mrs. Rhodes Bakery   1783 Cheshire Bridge Rd. N.E.

Campers and Coaches, Rental:

Campwagon Rentals Co.   2351 Roosevelt Highway, College Park

Caterers:

Cloudt's Food Store and Village Kitchen   1937 Peachtree Rd. N.E.
Northside Delicatessen   3209 Maple Drive, N.E.

Chairs Caned:

Johnson Chair Caning Shop   230 Carroll Ave. S.E.

China, Crystal and Silver:

Charles Willis, Inc.   3380 Peachtree Rd. N.E., and *Regency Hyatt House*   265 Peachtree Rd. N.E.

Conversation with a Mynah Bird?

H. G. Hastings   2350 Cheshire Bridge Rd. N.E. Ask for Joe.

Architect's rendering of Phipps Plaza across Peachtree from Lenox Square. Among New York stores represented are Saks Fifth Avenue, Lord & Taylor and Tiffany's.

Davison's, a Macy affiliate, on Peachtree Street in downtown Atlanta

CHEESE:

Cheese Shop   320 Pharr Rd. N.E.
Hoppe's Cheese Shop   Lenox Square Shopping Center

CRAFTS: (do-it-yourself)

The Craft Shack   2581 Piedmont Rd. N.E.
The Creative Cove   2218 Peachtree Rd. N.W.

DECORATIVES, POTTERY, GLAZED ENAMELS:

Radcliff Studios   Memorial Drive (U.S. 78) near Stone Mountain
The Signature Shop   3267 Roswell Rd. N.W. (also weavings and one-of-a-kind arts and crafts)

DOGS TRAINED:

Benno Stein Training School for Dogs   Dunwoody

Southeastern headquarters for Sears, Roebuck and Company sprawls on Ponce de Leon Avenue tract.

ENGRAVING (Social):

J. P. Stevens Engraving Co.   117 Peachtree St. N.E.

FABRICS:

Walter J. Penny, Inc.   3096 Roswell Rd. N.W.
Halpern's   Greenbriar and North DeKalb Shopping Centers

FURS (rental):

Atlanta Fur Service   1099 Ponce de Leon Ave.

FLOWERS:

Burch-Oliver   1181 Peachtree St. N.E.
Forresters, Inc.   2070 Cheshire Bridge Rd. N.E.
Harpers   1201 W. Peachtree St. N.E.
Irving Gresham   128 Peachtree St. N.W.

Fruit Gift Baskets:

Dial-a-Gift   2070 Cheshire Bridge Rd. N.W.; 207 Church St., Decatur

Furniture and Decoratives:

Atlanta Decorative Arts Center   351 Peachtree Hills Ave. N.E. (accompanied by interior decorators only)
Beverly Hall   2789 Piedmont Rd. N.E.
Biggs Antique Company   792 Peachtree St. N.E.
W. E. Browne Decorating Company   443 Peachtree St. N.E.
Edith Hills Interiors   351 Peachtree Hills Ave. N.E.
T. Gordon Little   2295 Peachtree Rd. N.E.
Rudolph-Sparks, Inc.   279 E. Paces Ferry Rd. N.E.

Furniture Restored and Reproduced:

E. R. Wilkerson, Inc.   2330 Piedmont Rd. N.E.
Trinity Furniture Shops   630 Angier Ave. N.E.

Furniture Repaired:

Carl A. Azar Furniture Shop   3231B Cains Hills Pl. N.W.

Furniture—Used:

The Flea Market   3063 Peachtree Rd. N.E.
Kimbrough's Furniture Mart   3183 Roswell Rd. N.E.

Garden Seeds:

L. H. Cottongim Seed Co.   94 Broad St. S.W.
Old Farm Greenhouse   3878 Buford Highway N.E. (instant gardens, hanging vegetable gardens, all in one basket)

Gifts:

Arthur Cobb, Inc.   3278 Peachtree Rd. N.E.
The Golden Rooster   3179 Peachtree Rd. N.E.
Stern's   1248 West Paces Ferry Rd. N.W.

GIFTS FROM OTHER WORLDS:

Madrid   2381 Piedmont Rd. N.W.

The Onion Dome   2265 Peachtree Rd. N.E.

Oriental Arts   1544 Piedmont Ave.

Oriental Bazaar   262 East Paces Ferry Rd. N.E.

Pier I Imports   3627 Peachtree Rd. N.E.

The Tokonoma Shop and Studio   672 Darlington Rd. N.E.

World Imports   Lenox Square Shopping Center

GOURMET GROCERIES:

Cloudt's Food Store and Village Kitchen   1937 Peachtree Rd. N.E.

Colonial Stores   Lenox Square and 43 West Paces Ferry Rd. N.W.

Matthews Super Markets   3457 Peachtree Rd. N.E. and 3663 Roswell Rd. N.E.

GROCERIES DELIVERED:

Hunt Fresh Foods   3771 Roswell Rd. N.E.

HARDWARE—DECORATIVE:

Atlanta Galleries   1405 Spring St. N.W.

HOUSEWARES:

Suburban House   Lenox Square Shopping Center

ICE CREAM:

Baskin and Robbins   Ansley Mall, 6064 Roswell Rd. N.E.; 35 B West Paces Ferry Road; 2581 Bolton Rd. N.W.; Peachtree Battle Shopping Center; 2144 North Decatur Rd., Decatur

JEWELRY:

Maier and Berkele, Inc.   173 Peachtree Rd. N.E.; 3225 Peachtree Rd. N.E.; 122 Clairmont Ave., Decatur

Claude S. Bennett   207 Peachtree Rd. N.E.; Lenox Square; N. DeKalb and Greenbriar Shopping Centers

Enclosed mall of Greenbriar Shopping Center protects customers from the weather.

KOSHER MEAT:

Katz Meat and Poultry Market   1048 N. Highland Ave. N.E.

LINGERIE, LINENS:

Frances Prince   3184 Peachtree Rd. N.E.

NURSERY AND LANDSCAPING:

Frank A. Smith   4020 Roswell Rd. N.W.
Hastings, H. G., and Co.   434 Marietta St., N.W.; 2360 Cheshire Bridge N.W.; 1205 Fairburn Rd. S.W.
Monroe Landscape and Nursery   2067 Manchester N.E.

LENDING LIBRARY:

Yellow Lantern   125 Rhodes Center N.W.

MUSIC TO YOUR OWN WORDS:

Perry Bechtel   55 Auburn Ave. N.E.

NEEDLEWORK (designed to your order):

Snail's Pace   480 E. Paces Ferry Rd. N.E.

ORIENTAL RUGS:

Y. Albert and Sons   2303 Peachtree Rd. N.E.
Robert Buckley and Co.   2800 Peachtree Rd. N.E.
Sharian, Inc.   368 W. Ponce de Leon Ave., Decatur

POODLE GROOMING:

Hays Patrick   1039 Marietta St.

PAN-DRESSED QUAIL:

South River Farms   53-14th St. N.E.

RECORDS:

Sallee's Record Shop   3084 Roswell Rd. N.W.

RENTAL CENTERS (practically anything—ask them):

Aaron Rents, Inc. 1173 W. Peachtree N.E.; 2881 Buford Highway N.E.; 1845 Piedmont Rd. N.E.; 2575 Chantilly Dr. N.E.

Abbey Rents, Inc. 3112 Piedmont Rd. N.E.

SHOES REMADE:

E. T. Bailey Shoe Repairing Candler Bldg.

SHOES (special widths and sizes):

Thompson, Boland and Lee 201 Peachtree St. N.E.; Lenox, Greenbriar, N. DeKalb and Cobb Shopping Centers

SILVER PLATING:

Simmons Plating Works, Inc. 409 Whitehall St. S.W.

TOPSOIL:

Atlanta Garden Center 4901 Buford Highway N.E.

USED CLOTHING:

Nearly New Shop 1005 Peachtree St. N.E.
Thrift House 3095 Peachtree Rd. N.E.

WALL SHELVING:

Forsgrens Wood Shop 316 Pharr Rd. N.E.

WINES:

Ansley Mall Bottle Shop Ansley Mall Shopping Center

WOOD FOR FIREPLACE:

Powers Woodyard 5990 Roswell Rd. N.W.

See the Whole State

UNTIL YOU'VE seen all of Georgia, you haven't quite got the picture.

The colony started out with a charter that encompassed all the land from the Atlantic to the Pacific and from the Savannah River to the South Seas.

Things didn't work out that way, but Georgia did end up as the largest state east of the Mississippi River. Its terrain and climate encompass seven of the nine climatic zones of the United States.

From old Brasstown Bald Mountain in the Blue Ridge chain of the Appalachians to the trembling earth of the Okefenokee Swamp, from Columbus at the edge of Alabama to Tybee Beach at the southern tip of South Carolina, is quite a swathe of territory.

If it is mountains, forests, plains or beaches you are looking for, this old 13th colony is the place to find them.

Let us outline five trips that will include all these and history too.

The Georgia Historical Commission is the state's agency that preserves treasures in historic sites. The Commission has placed 1700-odd bronze plaques throughout the state, marking all periods of Georgia history: Indian, pre-Colo-

The Little White House at Warm Springs, Georgia—the second home of Franklin Delano Roosevelt—where he died. Located southwest of Atlanta

The Trappist Monastery of the Holy Ghost at Conyers, Georgia. Located southeast of Atlanta

nial, Colonial, Antebellum and Confederate. These are to be found in almost every county.

The Commission maintains and is developing 15 historical sites, some of which are open to the public. A telephone call to 521-0057 before taking any junket will elicit excellent information about special places to see.

The Tourist Division, Georgia Department of Industry and Trade, P.O. Box 38097, Atlanta, Georgia 30334, will provide maps and more information on special trips.

The Tourist Division will also tell you whether the route you are planning will take you through any of the 29 remaining "Kissin' Bridges," ancient spans roofed with hand-rived shingles that once covered 250 streams in Georgia.

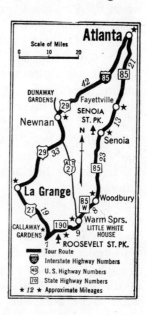

Southwest

Longest of the state's covered bridges, 149 feet, crosses Big Red Oak Creek in Meriwether County, where you may go on your first and shortest trip out of Atlanta to the southwest. This area is made memorable because it was Franklin Delano Roosevelt's home away from home and the place where he died in 1945, in the Little White House at Warm Springs.

The southwesterly trip will take you to Senoia State Park, Warm Springs, the Little White House, Callaway Gardens, Columbus and Fort Benning, LaGrange, Newnan and Hattie Dunaway Gardens, if you make it a round trip. If you are going only one way, Fort Benning would be the point of no return on this suggested tour.

SENOIA STATE PARK offers picnic facilities, swimming pool and playgrounds. When you continue south on 85W, the LITTLE WHITE HOUSE will come up soon toward the Pine Mountain area.

The cottage built for FDR in 1932 remains as it was when the President was in frequent residence. The simple furnishings are as they were. His special Model A Ford and Fala's dog chain are still there. You may see a newsreel and film reviewing the friendly years he spent with his Georgia neighbors while he sought relief from his paralysis in the healing therapies of the Warm Springs Foundation Hospital, which he inspired and helped finance.

From Warm Springs on Route 190 over the spine of Pine Mountain is a beautiful drive to the IDA CASON CALLAWAY GARDENS, one of the south's finest recreational areas.

The Callaway Gardens are a 2500-acre sanctuary for native plants, wild flowers and birds. There are eleven spring-fed lakes, white sand beaches and provisions for every aquatic interest including the Masters Water Ski Tournament, which has its headquarters at the Gardens. National water-skiing championships are held in August.

Facilities include family cottages, motels and a club-house with fine cuisine including such foods as quail with wine sauce and wild rice, sugar-cured ham with cherry sauce, and homemade bread. The Gardens operates a country store with a choice selection of old-fashioned jel-lies, preserves, candies, homemade breads and other tradi-tional rural fare.

COLUMBUS is the head of navigation on the Chattahoochee River. It is the home of Fort Benning, Infantry center for the United States and is also bristling with the history of hostile Indians, war, invasions, pistols at dawn and great industrial growth.

The Columbus Junior League conducts special tours on Wednesdays, beginning at 10 A.M. at the Georgia Welcome Center, to antebellum houses ranging from classic Greek revival to Italianate villas, an outstanding Indian collection at the Columbus Museum of Arts and Crafts, the Confederate Naval Museum, the Gunboat Muscogee, which was salvaged in 1963 after 98 years at the bottom of the river.

Twenty miles south of Columbus, at the crossroads of U.S. 27 and Georgia 27, is LUMPKIN, where residents have turned back the clock to the late 1820s and 1830s. Lumpkin was a stagecoach stop in Georgia's western wilderness, and one of its souvenirs of the past is Bedingfield Inn, an old stagecoach tavern. It has been handsomely restored, along with other buildings of historic consequence.

On the return trip through LAGRANGE, a major textile center, you may see beautiful antebellum mansions of the late 1890s.

There is also NEWNAN, a prosperous town not too far from Atlanta to be considered home by commuters, including former Governor Ellis Arnall, who has a law office in Atlanta.

The HATTIE DUNAWAY GARDENS, six miles north of Newnan, are a homage to the horticultural gift of the woman for whom they are named, who herself spent a lifetime converting 20 acres of red clay farmland to 20 acres of natural beauty with specimen plants so rare that botanists from all over the world visit the Gardens.

Return to U.S. 29, and back to Atlanta. You will have driven less than 250 miles.

CHICKAMAUGA &
CHATTANOOGA
NAT. MIL. PK.
Ringgold
FORT MTN.
Dalton ST. PK.
CHATTAHOOCHEE
NAT. FOR.
Spring Pl.
Chats-
worth
RESACA
CEM.
Calhoun
NEW
ECHOTA
Oostanaula R.
ETOWAH
INDIAN
MOUNDS
Cartersville
Allatoona
Lake
SPUR
KENNESAW MTN.
NAT.
BATTLEFIELD
PARK
Marietta
Atlanta

Tour Route
Interstate Highway Numbers
U. S. Highway Numbers
State Highway Numbers
12 Approximate Mileages

Scale of Miles
0   10   20   30   40

Northwest

This trip, a 240-mile circle, takes you northwest past Marietta, Kennesaw Mountain, Lake Allatoona, the Etowah Mounds, Cartersville, Calhoun, New Echota, Rome, Ringgold, Chickamauga and Chattanooga National Military Parks; then to Dalton, Spring Place and Chatsworth on your way back to Atlanta.

MARIETTA has a National Cemetery where 10,158 Union soldiers are buried beneath memorial monuments erected by their home states. A Confederate cemetery, somewhat removed, entombs 3,000 Confederate soldiers.

KENNESAW has hikers' trails which will prove that General Sherman was there. His cannons, trenches and markers are scattered all over the mountainside.

LAKE ALLATOONA covers 19,000 watery acres with docking facilities for all sizes of boats and plenty of space for water skiing. It is one of the few reservoirs in the nation dominantly populated with spotted bass.

The ETOWAH MOUNDS are mysterious prehistoric subjects of archaeological speculation, three miles west of U.S. 41 at Cartersville.

Close by, at ADAIRSVILLE, is Georgia's haunted castle, the crumbled remains of the Palladian Barnsley Gardens. The Civil War arrested Sir Godfrey Barnsley's plan to build this tribute to his young wife. Sir Godfrey's ghost is said to revisit, grieving for its lost glory.

The bronze statue of Sequoyah, the Indian scholar who invented the Cherokee alphabet in 1821, stands at the city limits of CALHOUN, which was once the heartland of the Cherokee nation. Three miles to the northeast on U.S. 41 and Route 22 to NEW ECHOTA will take you to the capital of the Cherokees from 1825 until they were forced to march westward.

If you go to ROME, you may pass Berry College, where Miss Martha Berry, a well-born young woman of beauty and property began a school for poor mountain children and devoted her life to proving the dignity and natural link between work and learning.

Georgia's Romans are proud of Darlington School for Boys, Shorter College and Thornwood School. Its people welcome September for the rousing Coosa Valley Fair, one of the few remaining great county fairs.

CHICKAMAUGA and CHATTANOOGA NATIONAL PARKS commemorate a Civil War battle which was the Confederacy's greatest victory in the west, though the Rebels were ultimately driven from the Chattanooga area. Markers tell the violent and valorous story.

Up this way is PLUM NELLY at the base of Lookout Mountain. Each year in October, painters from Chattanooga and residents thereabouts bring their art work, quilts, fancy work, for a much publicized exhibit. The show takes place at the peak of autumn glory in the mountains, which adds to its success.

A new organization, the Georgia Mountain Arts, Inc., is

The white marble for the Lincoln Memorial in Washington, D.C., came from these Cherokee marble pits at Tate Quarries in North Georgia.

being developed to promote arts and crafts in this corner of the state.

Returning via DALTON you will be in the center of a $1½ billion tufted-textile industry, where at least 50 percent of all the carpeting manufactured in the United States is produced. The industry grew out of an heirloom bedspread copied by Catherine Evans Whitener when she was a teen-ager in 1895. Confederate General Joseph E. Johnson headquartered here in 1864 at the Huff House. It was from here that Sherman began his campaign for Atlanta.

At SPRING PLACE on U.S. 76 out of Dalton, is the restored Vann House, home of Cherokee Chief Joseph Vann, who owned thousands of acres of land and 300 slaves. Chief Vann's house, the finest mansion in all the Cherokee Nation, has, among other things, carved mantels and secret hiding places.

Fort Mountain State Park at CHATSWORTH is about five miles to the east. So is Lake Conasauga, said to be the highest body of water in Georgia.

The scenery on this trip is a glory in itself. The country has the perfect balance of vista and height, mist and fog, sunshine and shadow and quaintness and austerity.

Northeast

The Northeastern mountain trip makes a circle around Lake Lanier, Gainesville, Dahlonega, Cleveland, Nacoochee, Helen, Unicoi Gap, Brasstown Bald, Hiawassee, Tallulah Gorge, Black Rock Mountain Park, lakes Burton, Seed, Rabun, Chatuge and Lakemont, Clarksville and Toccoa. Then back to Atlanta on Interstate 85.

An exciting plan is on the boards for the development of a cluster of islands consisting of 1,080 acres and 18 miles of shoreline at Lake Lanier. The Lake Lanier Islands Development Authority hopes to have the facility ready by 1975 to welcome as many as 3,500,000 visitors.

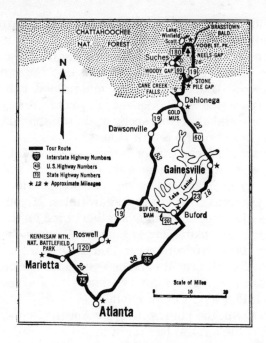

When you leave GAINESVILLE going north, you enter the rising heights of the Smokies. Don't try to hurry. If you pass up a mountain store, a festival or an antique shop, you may miss the pleasure of your life.

Enter this land at your peril. It is addictive.

Many people come here for a few hours, linger a day or so and eventually settle down in the shadow of old Brasstown Bald's 4,784-foot brooding eminence to contemplate mountain life at leisure.

All converts become handicrafters, weavers, artists, pottery makers, sorghum syrup cookers, herb gardeners, folklorists or candlemakers. They envelop themselves in piquant speech patterns with Elizabethan echoes, handed-down superstitions and ballads of the hill people, until they have completely forgotten the concerns that once engrossed them in the cities.

The least romantic thing one can say about Gainesville

is the most important economic fact to the townspeople. Gainesville is the world's poultry capital.

DAHLONEGA is Georgia's Gold Rush town, the earliest in America, where gold was discovered in 1828, and where for years the U.S. Government maintained a mint. You can still pan gold in Dahlonega, if you're greedy enough. We recommend that you spend your time gorging at the groaning board of the Smith House.

The patterned campus of North Georgia College has a serenity and order impressive to passersby.

You may hear about Dahlonega's prehistoric cairn, another mysterious memory of Indian times. If you pass the cairn, pay homage by tossing another stone on it.

Visit the Lumpkin County courthouse, circa 1836. The bricks of this structure were laid with mud containing particles of gold dust. It is being restored to vintage condition by the Georgia Historical Commission and the Georgia Mountain Planning Commission.

CLEVELAND, the point where the Appalachians spill into Georgia, is the natural habitat of the tupelo, Florida maple, black walnut, sweet gum and chestnut. The yellow poplars, sweet birch, dogwood, persimmons, oaks, beeches, sycamores, black gums, elms and basswoods create a magnificent mosaic in the fall, rising to a crescendo of color in mid-October.

This area is part of Chattahoochee National Forest, that 618,000-acre preserve flung across much of North Georgia. Intermingled with the public lands are thousands of privately owned acres. Rustic farmhouses nestling in curves, smoke curling from their chimneys, corn in neat shocks, present a peaceful demeanor against mountains which rise almost a mile high.

Cleveland's fall festival is usually held about October 15, with displays of Indian corn, apples, melon, sourwood honey, sorghum syrup and kitchen delicacies for sale.

Between Cleveland and HELEN are several recommended shopping stops. Burning Kilns, the pottery place of Bobby

Cleveland, turns out beautiful glazes; the Chestnut House of Treasures, seven miles north on Georgia 75 and 17, at Sautee-Nacoochee, offers individual handcrafts made by mountain people; the Old Sautee Store, also at Sautee-Nacoochee, has a shop of Nordic handicrafts.

The Nacoochee Valley Craft Shop on U.S. 129 between Cleveland and Helen has homemade jams, jellies, preserves, chutney and pickles put up by the skilled hands of Marianne Kidd.

At HELEN on Routes 17 and 75, the Tapawenga Trading Post features crafts of the Cherokee Indian Reservation and other mountain people.

The state parks in this region exploit stunning natural beauty: AMICALOLA, near Junio, has a 729-foot waterfall; BLACK MOUNTAIN, near Mountain City, is located on top of a 3,800-foot mountain, and CLOUDLAND CANYON, near Rising Fawn, contains Sitton's Gulch, known as Georgia's "Little Grand Canyon." UNICOI near Helen and VOGEL at Blairsville on Lake Trahlyta are colorful.

BRASSTOWN BALD has a Visitors' Information Center and an observation platform, operated by the U. S. Forest Service. On a clear day, four states may be seen from the top of Old Baldy. Sunset is a moment to be remembered.

CLAYTON is a summer resort to which stately families from middle and southern Georgia withdraw from the heat of August. Mrs. Edward North operates The Ham House, on U.S. 75, east of Clayton, where she purveys Georgia mountain country hams and assorted antiques.

HIAWASSEE, known as Georgia's Little Switzerland, holds its Georgia mountain fair in August. It features such rustic pleasures as a fiddler's contest, a mountain beauty contest, a rifle-shooting match, board splitting and an art exhibit; it also shows a mountain still in operation.

CLARKSVILLE, a museum in itself, present its Mountain Laurel Festival in May, a season of such fresh exuberance that it vies with autumn among mountain scenery addicts.

JARRETT MANOR, oldest house in Northeast Georgia, is

on U.S. 123, near Toccoa, and well worth seeing. It was built in 1784 by Major Jesse Walton, Revolutionary hero and Indian fighter, and served as frontier fort, stagecoach inn and early post office, as well as a plantation dwelling when Jarrett was the largest landowner in the county and raised his own silkworms.

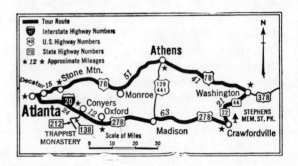

East

A different reflection of the past pervades a trip to the east, a mannerly, far more polished remembrance of the era of belles and beaux and great plantations.

We suggest you leave Atlanta on U.S. 278, driving in a large loop toward Covington, Madison and Crawfordsville to Augusta; north to Clark Hill Reservoir; on to Lincolnton, Washington (Wilkes County), Elbert County and Athens; then back on U.S. 29 and 78 through Monroe, Stone Mountain and Avondale.

MADISON, 50 miles from Atlanta, has an aura compounded of time, grace, old homes, old money and old assurance. This is a town General Sherman did not burn. Treasures including a bolt of material used for Confederate uniforms and white dancing slippers may be seen, along with many handsome columned old mansions, on the walking tours through Madison. These guided tours begin at 9 A.M. every weekend at the Morgan County Foundation Building on South Main Street. They may last until 5 P.M.

At CRAWFORDSVILLE, partially obscured by trees, stands

Liberty Hall, the antebellum home of Alexander H. Stephens, Vice President of the Confederacy and a former governor of Georgia. The Stephens home, which is neatly furnished with original furniture and reproductions, is now the focal point of a 1,175-acre state park. The Confederate Museum here contains relics, documents, diaries and personal effects of Mr. Stephens.

AUGUSTA is a busy, growing city, one of Georgia's largest, and may be appreciated for itself (not to mention that it is the scene of the Masters Golf Tournament each spring). It also possesses one of Georgia's most historic shrines, the famous Mackay House.

Mackay House, frontier Indian trading post and one of the finest examples of American Colonial architecture south of the Potomac, was the scene of terrible vengeance during the American Revolution. Thirteen Americans were hanged in the stairwell upon orders of wounded British Colonel Thomas Brown, who watched from his sickbed. Colonel Brown had previously been tarred and feathered.

Mackay House is furnished with classic antiques dating from the early 18th century; the second floor houses a collection of American Revolutionary war items.

Practically a whole lake serves as a shrine for Georgia's greatest revolutionary war hero, Elijah Clark. The lake of Clark Hill Dam, a tremendous impoundment of water reaching about 50 miles up the Savannah river, is part of the Elijah Clark Memorial State Park near LINCOLNTON.

You've probably heard of Tom Dooley ("Hang down your head, Tom Dooley"). Dooley's home is in this park too, down the road from the unreconstructed home of Clark.

WASHINGTON, Wilkes County, lives in its treasures. Forty white-columned mansions are occupied by their owners. The architecture of the town is Greek Revival—colonnades, widows' walks, herringbone brickwork, basement kitchens, great drawing rooms, withdrawing rooms. It was the scene of the last cabinet meeting of the Confederacy.

The Chamber of Commerce shows a few of these houses.

Tours with guides may be arranged with the Chamber office on Courthouse Square.

ELBERTON, county seat of Elbert County, is also a cluster of history, most of its houses being in mint repair, some viewable from the inside.

Elbert County proudly admits being the native heath of the rollicking gentlemen in the ballad "Old Dan Tucker"—he was the "grand old man who washed his face in a frying pan." Elbert County is also the birthplace of Nancy Hart, revolutionary heroine, for whom a state park in this area has been named.

ATHENS and SAVANNAH are probably Georgia's favorite cities; both have earned the affection. ATHENS is the site of the University of Georgia, oldest state-chartered university in the nation, with an enrollment of more than 12,000 students.

The town is a three-dimensional archive by itself, and the best way to appreciate it is to take one of two tours operated by the Chamber of Commerce. In addition to some grand houses, among them the sumptuous Benjamin H. Hill House, now the home of the president of the University, and the Stephen Upson house, which has silver doorknobs, you may see the second generation of the Tree That Owns Itself. This white oak owns the land within a radius of eight feet of its roots, a claim stoutly made with a strong chain enclosure.

Not far from Athens, at WATKINSVILLE, is the Eagle Tavern, operated as an inn from 1801 until 1906. A 17-room tavern and store built with broad, square nails and grooved planks, Eagle Tavern is now in custody of the Georgia Historical Commission.

When you head back through MONROE, Stone Mountain and AVONDALE, you will be well advised to stop at each place and do some exploring. Monroe, like Madison, where you began this trip, is flavored with history.

You have already been introduced to Stone Mountain. Who knows? The 610-bell carillon may be ringing just for

you as you drive past. The bells ring at noon, 4 and 8 P.M.,
and on Sundays at 1, 3, 5 and 8 P.M.

South

This trip will be longer and more varied than the others,
reaching farther into the past. It points back to the explora-
tions of De Soto, de Luna and Ribaut, to the opening of
Georgia as a colony, to the first churches of the state, to the
emergence of the state itself. It sweeps from the Piedmont
ridge on which Atlanta stands through the fertile heart-
lands to the Atlantic seashore, from clay and giant pines to
sand and moss-draped cypress, from the foothills of a lin-
gering mountain chain to the marshes of Glynn. These are
the marshes poet Sidney Lanier called "candid and simple
and nothing withholding and free."

We suggest a long drive to the southeast as far as St.
Mary's, almost to the Florida line, across toward the southwest and a swing back to Atlanta. It will be easier to consult
your own map, since many of the points of interest are
off the major routes.

Generally, you might go through Conyers to Covington,
down through Oconee National Forest and Lake Sinclair
to Milledgeville, over to Macon and the Ocmulgee National
Monument, thence to Savannah and down the Atlantic
coast to Darien, Sea Island, St. Simons, Brunswick, Jekyll,
over to Waycross and the Okefenokee Swamp, west to
Thomasville, up through Albany, Blakely, Andersonville,
Montezuma, Fort Valley and back to Atlanta.

The Trappist Monastery of the Holy Ghost is at CON-
YERS, 30 miles southeast of Atlanta. You are welcome to
visit this 20th-century ecclesiastic retreat where 100
hooded monks work and pray in almost utter silence under
vows of poverty, chastity, obedience.

The Abbey of Our Lady of the Holy Ghost, 6 miles off
Highway 78, was built by the monks' own hands, as was

the entire monastery, even to fashioning the leaded glass and the stained-glass windows. People of all faiths are received warmly. Those wishing to spend a few days of solitude and contemplation within the quiet walls are welcome to do so.

The monks grow and make their own food. Their gift shop sells delicious homemade wholewheat bread from 8 A.M. to 8 P.M. daily.

COVINGTON has many old homes. It was an established community when Atlanta was a brawling traders' village.

MILLEDGEVILLE was the capital of Georgia from 1807 to 1868. Milledgeville's old Governor's Mansion is considered a perfect example of Georgian architecture. It has been furnished throughout by gifts from Georgians and is open to the public Tuesday through Saturday from 10 A.M. to 4 P.M., and on Sundays from 2 to 5 P.M.

MACON, which is Georgia's geographical mid-point, is a mixture of ancient and modern. It might be a good idea to get a tour booklet and free map from the Macon Chamber of Commerce, 640 First Street.

You can see Indian culture in the restored earth lodge and the giant mounds at Ocmulgee National Monument, a preserve of 638 acres along Routes U.S. 80 and 129 on the northern edge of the city.

One can sense Macon's link with the Colonial period in Fort Hawkins, on a hillside on the north bank of the Ocmulgee River. The fort was built in 1806 upon authority of President Thomas Jefferson.

Macon was not in the path of Sherman and his fire brigade. Many prewar structures still exist, including the Cannon Ball House, built in 1853, an authentic example of Greek Revival architecture.

The great house of Macon is the Johnston Hay House, 934 Georgia Avenue, built in Italian Renaissance style, with 24 rooms, frescoed ceilings, Carrara marble mantels, a 500-pound hand-carved rosewood door with silver hinges, and furnishings in exquisite taste including Waterford chandeliers and Savonnerie carpets.

The poet-musician Sydney Lanier was born in Macon in 1842. There is a monument to his memory.

Take a look at the Citizens and Southern "Crystal Palace" Bank. It is pure gay nineties, including flowered rugs, red walls and fancy chandeliers agleam with polished old brass.

Be sure to see the new George Beattie mural in the lobby of the United States Post Office and Federal Building in Macon. Mr. Beattie is an Atlanta artist. The mural covers 400 square feet and depicts the history of Macon and Middle Georgia.

SAVANNAH has transcendent charm. It was one of the earliest planned cities in America, with a series of public squares insuring order and harmony.

Savannah, of course, was the birthplace of Georgia, where Oglethorpe brought his colonists; where President George Washington visited; where Tomochichi, Chief of the Yamacraw Indians was buried; where Juliette Gordon Low, founder of the Girl Scouts of America, was born.

Mad Anthony Wayne, Casimir Pulaski, Marquis de Lafayette, the Irish patriot Robert Emmett, General Nathaniel Greene, the infamous Captain Flint of Treasure Island fame—all were there.

One of the better restorations runs along the riverfront, where you will find flavorful dining spots. This was a project led by Atlanta and Savannah banker Mills B. Lane and his family.

We suggest you have a meal at the Pirates' House in Trustee's Garden, which you will be shown early in the visit to Savannah.

South from Savannah on U.S. 17 is Midway Church, long a shrine in the village of Midway. Some 200 years ago it was the religious center for the Puritan settlers of this section. Two signers of the Declaration of Independence from Georgia, Lyman Hall and Button Gwinnett, were among its communicants.

Fort Frederica and Christ Episcopal Church are two musts at ST. SIMONS. The church has been here for 232 years almost without interruption, having been established as a mission of the Church of England in 1736.

St. Simons and SEA ISLAND are part of Georgia's Golden Isles, which lie in marshy frames near the Florida Coast. Sea Island is a pleasure resort of national importance; the Cloister is one of the ranking luxury holiday hotels.

JEKYLL ISLAND, now a state-owned public resort, was once the private playground of the world's wealthiest men: Vanderbilt, Astor, Gould, McCormick, Rockefeller, Armour, Biddle, Goodyear, Macon—100 of them in all. Its climate was perfect; for 60 years no uninvited foot ever stepped on the island. It now has several motels and an excellent beach.

Perched in the extreme southeastern corner of the state, ST. MARY'S, on Georgia 41, was once a U. S. Customs port in the days when Spain ruled Florida. The community flourished for 75 years as a deep-water port and playground of coastal planters. Smuggling was big business. St. Mary's has legends, memories, ghosts and plans for the future. Let a St. Maryan tell you about it.

"The Land of the Trembling Earth" was the Seminole description of the Okefenokee Swamp, the largest freshwater swampland preserve in the nation and the most unusual natural wonderland in America.

This eerie, sentient water jungle, asplash and alive with the sounds of alligators, snakes, fish, waterfowls and owls begins a few miles south of Waycross and extends for 40 miles into Florida. It covers a 700-square-mile expanse.

The Okefenokee is now operated as a park. Its forbidden mysteries, which once only adventurers, trappers, hunters and lumbermen dared explore, are open to the public. The entrance is eight miles south of Waycross on U.S. 1 and 23. You may angle for 50 species of fish if you have the patience to hold a pole or cast a line. Watch out for your dog here. Alligators love them . . . to eat.

The best antidote to the primordial atmosphere of the Okefenokee is a trip west to gracious old THOMASVILLE, where each year the rose upstages the gentry. There are plenty of both. Thomasville has something like 150,000 rosebushes, all trained to burst into ecstasy on cue each year about April 19, which is also the signal for livestock parades, calf scrambles, a Rose Queen pageant, a golf tournament, a ball, a horse show, and plantation tours throughout the week.

Thomasville has as many acres in plantation estates as it has roses. This is where the rich of the world come to get away from it all, to hunt and ride and be treated like kings. Jacqueline Kennedy Onassis and Lord Harlech were among those who visited here in 1968.

You are headed back to Atlanta now, but you ought to stop at ALBANY to see Radium Springs. This was once called "Shy Water" by the Creeks. The springs are of unknown depth, flow at a rate of 70,000 gallons a minute and keep a constant temperature of 68 degrees Fahrenheit. Indians believed in their curative powers.

You ought to go to BLAKELY where apparently the Kolomoki Indians were planning master communities and cities as far back as eleven centuries ago. The Kolomoki Indian mounds, which have been extensively dug by archaeologists, have unfolded villages, temples, plazas, which were once inhabited by 2,000 people.

Eight mounds at Blakely and a permanent exhibit show how the Indians lived between A.D. 800 and 1200.

ANDERSONVILLE Cemetery and Prison Park on Georgia 29 is an enclave of sadness. Heartbreak, failure and a lost cause are evoked by the monument to 13,000 Union soldiers who died there as prisoners in 1864. The story of Andersonville was told by MacKinlay Kantor in his book of the same name.

Ten miles north is MONTEZUMA, peach heartland which has now become a Georgia colony for Mennonites. The inviting land of Macon County has been further smoothed by the quiet Mennonites who, with work, piety and communal purpose, have built their own gentle society around their small Amish church.

Flower lovers, especially camellia addicts, should not

miss Massee Lane, Dave Strother's camellia showplace a few miles north of Montezuma, between Marshallville and Fort Valley. Strother has thousands of varieties of camellias, the largest collection in the world. He has never sold a plant nor a blossom. His gardens are free and open every day of the year from sunrise to sunset.

On to the north, on U.S. 23 at INDIAN SPRINGS near Jackson, is the McIntosh House, called by some the most historic house in Georgia. It was there, on February 12, 1825, that a treaty was signed with the Creeks ceding all Creek territory in Georgia and Alabama in exchange for lands farther west. The treaty served as a death warrant for General William McIntosh, chief signer for the Creeks, himself a half-breed Creek. Within three months his scalp was suspended from a pole in a public square at Otuskee, a Creek village.

McIntosh House is open only in the summer months. It has no heating system.

Your next stop will be Atlanta where, heating systems or not, your welcome will always be warm.

Christ Episcopal Church at St. Simons, established as a mission in 1736.

ABOUT THE AUTHORS

Doris Lockerman and Patricia LaHatte have been observing and recording Atlanta for many years as colleagues on the staffs of its newspapers.

Mrs. LaHatte, a graduate of the High Museum of Art, has been Art Editor of the *Atlanta Journal Magazine* and Picture Editor of the *Atlanta Journal*. She has been Promotion Manager of the *Atlanta Journal and Constitution* for 15 years. She has been chairman of the Forward Atlanta Advertising and Promotion Committee for the Atlanta Chamber of Commerce and is President-Elect of the International Newspaper Promotion Association.

Mrs. Lockerman, who spent five years on the city desk of the *Chicago Tribune*, has been Associate Editor of the *Atlanta Constitution* and reporter and columnist for both the *Atlanta Constitution* and the *Atlanta Journal*. She has been Public Information Director for Lockheed Aircraft Corporation's Georgia facility and has conducted a daily television program for Station WAGA-TV.

Mrs. Lockerman is the wife of Atlanta attorney Allen E. Lockerman, Jr. Her community interests range from membership on the Citizens Advisory Committee for Urban Renewal to the Board of Visitors of Emory University and the Women's Association of the Atlanta Symphony. She is the mother of two sons, grandmother of five.

Each of the authors has been cited as Woman of the Year in Business in Atlanta.